WITHOUT ANESTHESIA

Aleš Debeljak
Without
Anesthesia

New and Selected Poems

A KAREN & MICHAEL BRAZILLER BOOK
PERSEA BOOKS / NEW YORK

The translations by Chistopher Merrill from *Anxious Moments*, copyright © 1994, and *The City and the Child*, copyright © 1999, appear with the generous permission of White Pine Press.

Thanks to the editors of the following journals, in which some of the translations in this book previously appeared: *American Poetry Review, Boston Review, The Case of Slovenia, Circumference, Coal Hill Review, Double Vision: Four Slovenian Poets, Guernica, Kenyon Review, Harvard Review, LIT, The New Republic, P.E.N. International Review* (UK), *Parthenon West Review, Poetry International, The Prose Poem: An International Journal, Prague Literary Review* (Czech Republic), *Redlands Review, Seneca Review, Slope, Southwest Review, Third Coast, Verse* and *Words Without Borders.*

A number of poems appeared in the limited-edition book *Sliver of Salt* (Brooklyn: Filter, 2008), edited and designed by Sara Parkel. "Cast Vote" appeared in *The New European Poets*, edited by Kevin Prufer and Wayne Miller (Saint Paul: Graywolf, 2008).

Translations by Andrew Zawacki were supported by a Slovenian Ministry of Culture Translation Grant and a Hugh Kenner Research Travel Award from the Department of English at the University of Georgia.

Thanks, too, to Judith Bishop, Brian Henry, and Tomaž Šalamun.

Persea Books, Inc.
853 Broadway
New York, NY 10003

Library of Congress Cataloging-in-Publication Data

Debeljak, Ales, 1961-
  Without anesthesia : new & selected poems / Ales Debeljak ; edited by
Andrew Zawacki. -- 1st ed.
    p. cm.
  "A Karen & Michael Braziller book."
  ISBN 978-0-89255-365-5 (original trade pbk. : alk. paper)
  I. Zawacki, Andrew, 1972- II. Title.
  PG1919.14.E28W58 2011
  891.8'416--dc22
                    2010047641

Designed by Lytton Smith
First edition
Printed in the United States of America

Contents

Under the Waterline

[Introduction]

"Your hand's half-raised," Aleš Debeljak has written, "to greet or wave goodbye, like this:"

The phrase—the *poem*—ends not with a period, as one might expect, but with a colon, the punctuation behaving like a passage or sluice, allowing the language to flow through, to gush past itself, into a silent space where the imagination is invited to visualize that hand—frail or reluctant, in its halfway gesture—hailing hello or bidding adieu. According to German poet and translator Paul Celan, one of Debeljak's major influences, a poem is always en route, moving ceaselessly toward a possible reception by someone else. There can be no poetry, properly speaking, without a reader to welcome its coming (even if it keeps advancing, passing by, and doesn't stay). A door ajar, a message in a bottle, a poem clears an area across which it calls to the strangeness of somebody else to be acknowledged. It is giving and hospitable both.

If readers of Aleš Debeljak's poetry find this generous notion continuously affirmed throughout his work, they also encounter an oeuvre fraught with rifts. Debeljak's earliest poems, composed when his homeland of Slovenia had just emerged from Josep Broz Tito's reign as Marshal of Yugoslavia, are marked by solitude and acute metaphysical anxiety—not fear per se, but worry that knows no object. This anguish, a fracturing of identity as global as it was personal, seemed to eerily presage the Third Balkan War, when "our century," Debeljak lamented in his essay-memoir *Twilight of the Idols*, "died in Sarajevo." The traumas of that conflict's ethnic cleansing and sniper-fire, international pussyfooting and eventual disintegration, erupted on the edges of Slovenia in 1991. After centuries of dominance by foreign powers (Hapsburg, Austro-Hungarian, Napoleonic, Axis) and subsequent autonomy within the Socialist Federal Republic of Yugoslavia, Slovenia finally gained independence after a Ten Day War with the Serb-led Yugoslav army—during which Debeljak served as a CNN field interpreter—two years after the Velvet Revolutions across Central and Eastern Europe. Newly democratic, eager to participate in the transnational marketplace, Slovenia would join NATO and the European Union in spring 2004 (events that have made Debeljak—a measured proponent of collective identity in his country of only two million—understandably cautious).

Ever concerned with the inadequacies of language and fascinated by both foreign and familiar geographies, Debeljak's early poems orient themselves by the intimacy of love and family. "Because we were no longer the babbling step-children of Coca Cola and Marx, but rather their uncertain hostages," he recalled of the tumultuous 1980s, when many established writers became the puppets of party politics and purveyors of an unimaginative *poésie engagée*, "we grew even more inspired by the modest pleasures of lonely people living in barren rooms, and our writing became the quandary of describing those lives." Equally personal and introspective, his most recent books are characterized by a more sustained engagement with history, literary and national heritage, and the frequently invoked "tribe." Poetry, to evoke Celan again, is a handshake, and Debeljak's poems have constantly, capably reached across state borders, linguistic cacophony, religious and cultural clash, and artistic genealogies, to make contact with an array of other coasts. "To dictate," he writes, "in a simple way, my last will and testament: for you the world will be / an open hand." His study of post-Communist Europe is quite appropriately titled *The Hidden Handshake*, and he has repeatedly referred to his collaboration with several American translators, including this one, as "four-handed," as though implying that all translation were inevitably co-translation.

Debeljak's penchant for nomadism seems to have begun at the beginning: He was born in a rented room—no hot water, common toilets for several apartments—in Ljubljana on Christmas day 1961. His Catholic parents, barely into their twenties, had moved from the countryside. Debeljak went to grammar school in Prule, a neighborhood on the banks of the Ljubljanica, and as several later lyrics reveal he spent his childhood in close contact with the river and its corridor of weeping willows, designed by architect Jože Plečnik as allusions to washerwomen. Afterward, Debeljak matriculated at the Šentvid Gymnasium, a four-year liberal arts high school in the Central European tradition. Designed to accommodate student athletes, the school catered especially to skiers and ski jumpers. Debeljak qualified in judo, however, training five times a week and competing on weekends with the Ljubljana-based club Olimpija. Twice a champion in Slovenia and once a vice-champion of the former Yugoslavia, Debeljak made the national judo team for under-16s. When he was injured during an international tournament in Koblenz, Germany, his attention and energy turned to writing. If not for that injury, Debeljak likes to joke, he might have become a Phys Ed teacher.

After graduating in May 1980 (the very month that Marshal Tito died) Debeljak took up comparative literature and philosophy at the University of Ljubljana, completing his undergraduate studies in 1985. He won several national student awards that year for *Imena smrti*, as well as a pan-Yugoslav prize for young artists and athletes (as did the tennis star Monika Seles). During his undergraduate years, he edited the student bi-monthly *Tribuna*, which under his watch was censored and twice banned—punishments he considered a great compliment for that bustling era of the decaying Communist regime.

Visiting the U.S. for the first time in summer 1985, Debeljak spent two months on a Greyhound bus, going coast to coast on the open road. Surveying the landscape and falling in with a medley of folks, everywhere attentive to American "Kulchur," he swore to return some day. Because, in his words, he "didn't have the guts" to wait tables in New York City while pursuing poetry on the side, Debeljak continued the academic route. He enrolled at Syracuse University, in the Maxwell School of Citizenship and Public Affairs, earning a Ph.D. in social theory in 1993. His dissertation, *Reluctant Modernity*, would become his first critical volume to appear in the States and those years in New York would prove crucial in forming relationships with American writers, among them Agha Shahid Ali, Tess Gallagher, Richard Jackson, David Rivard, Charles Simic, and David Wojahn. He married Erica Johnson, author of the memoir *Forbidden Bread* and translator of the late Slovenian poet Dane Zajc, and the couple relocated to Ljubljana, where they raise a trio of children. Today the family lives on Zvezna Ulica, a banal fact that nonetheless resonates importantly with Debeljak: initially an allusion to the now defunct Yugoslav federation, Union Street, as it's translated, "hints at one of the most crucial determinants of the human condition," namely, "shared life" and community, "the possibility of understanding and respect for 'the other.'"

Debeljak is a relentless traveler, by default and by design. His cities include Vienna and Venice, Chicago and Krakow, Barcelona and Budapest, Paris and Prague—not to mention Sarajevo, Belgrade, Zagreb. "I would like to become myself a map of the city," he claimed in an article on the republic of letters, "a written page, a thin cobweb through which older and dimmer biographies and urban chronicles shine." No city, needless to say, is dearer to him than Ljubljana, whose main square features a bold statue of national poet France Prešeren—who wrote in Slovenian, not in the German that dominated nineteenth-century Central Europe— gazing across at his muse and unrequited love, Julia. A medieval castle visible on a nearby hill, downtown Ljubljana is defined by the elegant Tromostovje, or Three Bridges (referred to in the poem "Drowned Love") and by the Dragon Bridge with its four copper guardians. The striking, pink Franciscan Church of the Annunciation is flanked by an expansive array of café and restaurant terraces, farmers' markets and handicraft stalls, and hipster bars whose lights and groovy music swathe the river after dark. The Baroque central pharmacy might be mistaken for an opera house, but the Slovenian national opera—along with the university and law faculty, national library and art museum, major cultural centers and publishing houses, Tivoli Park, and the writers' union—are all just a casual walk from city center. "I came to realize," Debeljak recalls of his formative treks, "that a true cosmopolitan is one who can confidently move about the world without forgetting his or her national origins and ethnic background."

His mobility and malleability among genres is further evidence of Debeljak's commitment to transit and transition. He is at home in literary criticism no less than in poetry ("Critical essays," he claims, "are a kind of intellectual poetry"), as well as in translation, the anecdote, and cultural commentary, whether printed or presented in a public debate. *Without Anesthesia* makes evident that Debeljak has experimented with a variety of forms, though its mainly excerpted arrangement can't fully adhere to the individual volumes' respective architectures. This diversity, across books, is in counterpoint to the scrupulous consistencies within them. Usually composed in intensive bursts of a few short, concentrated weeks, Debeljak's poems are often structured in series, as their ideas, emotions, and images clarify one another, protract and backtrack, surge, settle like so much dust to be kicked up again.

Hence the poems' many hellos and goodbyes, and his collections' vacillating dedications: Each of Debeljak's poetry volumes is dedicated variously to an indeterminate "you," beginning, with piquant ambiguity, with "for who else but you" (*Names of the Dead*), and followed by "for you" (*Dictionary of Silence*), "for you, maybe" (*Anxious Moments*), "for both of you" (*The City and the Child*), "for you, almost unconditionally" (*Unended*), and finally "for you, this time without hesitation" (*Under the Waterline*). It would probably be wrong to think of this oscillation as dialectical, for Debeljak is not one to attempt to bring the discordant world into inauthentic harmony. Still, it is hard not to wonder: who is the "you" he signals? Given the pronounced sensuality in the later writing especially, sometimes we figure a lover is near. Unlike English, the Slovenian language features a dual case, a way of saying "we" and meaning just you and me; not surprisingly for an author so keen on company and admittedly split in half, duality is one of Debeljak's natural habitats. Other times, "you" is most likely the poet's wife and their newborn daughter. Elsewhere, the second person—be it singular or plural—may very well be "I," as the poems issue directives to the poet himself, whether instructions or promises, encouragement or reprimand. Perhaps Debeljak is conversing with the many figures his poems salute, from Samuel Beckett, for whom the early "Chronicle of Melancholy" is written, to Danilo Kiš, whose tenacity in "defying both the rigidity of nationalist navel-gazing and the blithe nonsense of 'global citizenship'" made him a "writer-hero" to the young Debeljak, "the most noble accomplishment of the Balkan imagination," "my master." The poems could equally be talking to fellow citizens like Tomaž Šalamun or Edvard Kocbek, unless the addressee is more vague, more available than any proper name: "This poem is for you, anonymous," he says in *Dictionary of Silence*, failing to clarify whether it's the poem or its audience that's nameless. And, unabashed, Debeljak's recent poems speak explicitly, if sometimes tentatively, to a "lord," evoking not so much the orthodox Christian god as that Romantic principle of creativity and transcendence proffered by Rilke's "Autumn Day," with its urgent appeal, "Lord, it is time." For Debeljak, too, is concerned with shadows darkening a sundial, fruit ripening on the vine at the dénouement of summer, the barren paths of a homelessness that is existential and socio-political alike. These are poems of pilgrims and refugees, anchorites and innocent prisoners, of internecine war and ontological strife, of the body's curves and the landscape's vertigos.

As readers we are overtly invited to listen, to look, while these poems are ushered outward. So "you" is also *you*, as in, "tell me the lyrics of your song, I want to sing with you."

Andrew Zawacki

[FROM] **DICTIONARY OF SILENCE**

for you

Biography of Sleep

1.

Shadows are thickening, the long backs of hills plunge
into the ocean's waves, the drone of a trumpet solo
is heard. Perhaps it comes from a transistor—
Somewhere at the edge of the visible world the hidden

power of melancholy is lost in the quicksand of Maghreb.
—Noon throbs metallic. Veterans sleep in wicker rocking
chairs. Their shoes' soft leather smells perhaps of resin
and of punitive journeys—Ripe fruit lies in the burnt

grass of the garden. The white walls of small houses
shiver from the heat, lethargy corrodes the officer's liver.
And turns it into a catalog of plants—One of them
recites Dante. Many deaths slowly gather in him.

2.

Clock hands have been still for years. Young roe deer
are frozen in lithographs. —Reports continue. —And
fermented fruit goes to the head: in weightless dizziness
there is a mirage. Which multiplies with recent encounters

with the theory of poison. Many times. No surprise: memory
melts like wax. The magnetic circle of crime is now stronger
than gravity. Nothing unusual. If pigeons flutter in dreams,
they retreat at once into oblivion. —This instant, when the air

trembles with fervor: all places trick the memory on times
passed, variations of murder, the symmetry of slow deaths.
All of these. And the human trace is tattooed with a green snake
head, burning with a wish to break through the sound barrier.

3.

This poem is for you, anonymous. Irritable and ill from
monotonous waiting for some cry still wandering through
seasons. And you don't write a diary. No one has, no one
like you. You're left to yourself. And to nostalgia for the future.

In your own way you will endure refugee camps and part from
beautiful ornaments in secessionist architecture. On titmouse
feathers you might lay eyes, the brief glimmering of weapons.
And your solitary whistle. Which lasts. Long. It will harden into elegy.

You can do nothing about this. So it must happen. Then despair
murmuring softly in us. That's the point. You can drink six bottles,
but you will not revive your own face in the mirror of a stranger's
memory. You will be single and alone until the end. Surely.

4.

Banks, flags, ships, holidays, cock fights, epaulets,
copper engravings of English horses, dead guards
and elite divisions. All this slides by. Disappears
like talk during an afternoon slumber. —

Face it. Arrival and a desolate scene are the same thing.
Instead of a planted tree and pages of a will only a name
remains, which someone entered in a dictionary. Nothing
more. Oh, perhaps someone for a moment remembers

the metamorphosis from pale to purple: like in old times with
lords. Otherwise it is really nothing. —Rip the crumpled
carnation off the chest, lean over the geometric granite
cubes, exhale. Now. Like those in the Stammheim Prison.

5.

At the border of lip and tongue, someone is counting days
to a strong earthquake, which Halley's Comet did not predict.
And bird catchers are emptying full traps, and family
homes sink into the mud. As from afar, grape leaves

scorched with *Peronospora* gently fall off the fronts
of houses. And the spears of white hunters unerringly
find the softness of loins and bellies: I would like to place
the last period. Listen, there is no rhetorical figure

of eternity. Behind a closed window some long vowel foretells
an influx of sorrow, which laps meekly in anguished people.
A thick haze settles on all sides and the room expands.
Under a railway embankment the two of you are lost in a slow fuck.

6.

To survive all that persists in evident harmony.
To be snow on a warm palm, which will freeze from
the weight of silvery crystals. To be a letter in Sanskrit.
Buckwheat honey. To be less than eternity and confidential

documents. To become poppies, tobacco leaves, a flat
landscape. A word which no one can repeat properly.
To rustle to someone like a rhyme from a sonnet
and instantly sink into disorder. To be absurd bird

chatter echoing in all the rooms like a melody. To be vast
fields, blues in forty-year-olds' memories. To survive
the anguish of a space that constricts like an animal's pupil.
That attacks with dreadful force and settles its belated debt.

7.

Under horizons of wet flocks it could have been otherwise.
Perhaps neighbors would leave him in the room for at least
three days. So that the air might lie heavily on his eyes, open
wide to the hunt and flight. And to nostalgia, which no one

among them can shake off. So that the thin song of death would
echo in his ear. And the casual droning of bees would close the circle.
But I don't believe it. In the people endlessly wandering, some
map is always rioting beyond the edges of these lines.

And it borders on the unbearable. So that the premonition
of a cuckoo's muffled singing clearly breathes in them.
And in their liver burns brute strength, which in the presence
of a woman turns into yearning. With it comes the smell of cinnamon.

Without Anesthesia

Naked, alone and heartless
I stand. There is no center of the world.
My weeping cleanses nothing,
my body isn't my property,
the salt irritates the skin.

Brane Bitenc, "I Watch Your Going"

1.

Things are empty. Nothing's in them. As if they're the fruit
of a failed plan. The landscape lies in water, greened
by a certain plant. It is eclipsed by the horizon line.
Filled with emptiness, which frightens everyone.

This morning smells perhaps of jasmine tea. But this still
does not mean that it has some sense. You can continue
with walks by the shore, it changes nothing. All
that captures your gaze is no more than a bitter mirage.

Which recalls snapshots of experiences you already know.
In no way do you want to find a place for things. Which last
longer than your fantasy, hopes, secrets. You are surrounded
by things. This isn't so bad. Only they are reliable. Only they.

2.

Powerless like flatlands, which never drown
at the horizon, and now still more: like for instance
water in the lake, which worries about evening
and does not spill over the bank. Powerless, you long

for death, you wait, watch, breathing secretly. Or what?
The expected figure does not appear in the shallows. Not
for a second, perhaps less. Seeing and hearing are too much:
under the surface of the gathered water is little depth,

like in the memory of a calm motion of a pregnant woman
one morning on your street. The force of gravity
is enough, you realize. And the names, days, and nights,
the lives of unknown generations. It's all too much.

3.

It is time. Say what was once already said.
So that there will be no misunderstanding. Begin
where you want. More than now you won't tolerate.
In a bird's takeoff from the water's surface, there's

already a fall. You too will lose nothing. You keep
as much as you give. Fleeing in a foreign tongue
is longing for silence. Whose bodies do not fray,
because you know them from the inside.

Because only people die, not their silence.
But flocks of starlings returning home are loud.
You'll have to raise your voice. Speak now! Say
how you keep quiet and become the breath of all people.

4.

Enough words. Better to doze off. Above me wild geese,
dry cough and embers in me. —A gust of wind spins
the weathervane. In the end I stayed. It is the right
time that I become the acoustics of silence, a secret

ongoing dialogue. I won't be anybody's cry anymore,
crystallized in amber. The stars are cold, people
turn on lights in flats. Night's ultrasound goes across
the world. What can I still expect, what can I still give?

I remembered the rhythm of physical pain with which
the world begins every day. I know the illusion of images
and old texts, I would like to be alone again.
Like the baby crying when separated from his mother.

5.

A shudder shakes you, and despair: every thing in your room
and anywhere else, every one has its own name. Vertigo
fills your days, motionlessly you observe the dim image
of the television, empty yards, the backs of books and of records,

narrow stairways: the desolate sky repeats this despair
on thin ice, spread bluish across a puddle. Worthless
shapes of clouds, so little love! With lips more timid
than you think, you slip reluctantly across the stillness

of things. And the pulsing of blood does not disturb the silence,
you still endure it alone. Like your pain that you don't want
to be what you are: the things that last without you.
For them you are already as dead as a crumpled rose.

6.

The hardly discernible flickering of air, mimosa fields,
incredible scent of a certain root, the glow of the lamp,
she holds in a raised hand: what noise does she hear now
around her head, half vanished in the evening twilight?

A cold sweat flows over her forehead and runs into open eyes.
Burned by the salty fluid. Her view darkens. More and more,
the silence grows. A fire from dry grasses is lit beneath
her feet. In an instant she will need to forget pleasant days.

On her lips, too, you will not discern the dry print of sorrow
that gathers. The earth still spins ahead, possibly nothing
happened. The forest quiet, all the paths are in front of her.
She stands still and listens to the sound of emptiness.

7.

Damp asphalt. And the placid, timeless stream of minerals
in the hill and valley. Unknown to you, casually silent
like lichens in the forests of distant northern regions.
An ordinary phrase from a conversation lasts forever.

And contains four, five words. Which perhaps only the melody of love
drowns out. —The dial on the phosphorescent clock glows. The date
of your helplessness. Long ago you predicted that you'd never find
the right translation for it. —If you could invent a language

without verbs, you could live longer, perhaps. And would lay down
all the weight of passing in a never spoken touch. Thus it will boil
in the skull and somewhere else. The face will fossilize.
And on the retina of the eye, a blind spot is left like Moby Dick.

[FROM] **ANXIOUS MOMENTS**

for you, maybe

Elegies from the North

Earth. Red earth. And tall grass as far as you can see. You're pressed to the ground. Hidden from unwanted glances. Utterly still. A quail by your ear. Are you turning into stone? No: you're just listening to shadows fall over cornfields. A bead of sweat—a tear?—slides down your cheek. In the distance a mountain rises steeply. Naked. Without trees or flowers. Imprinted on the sharp-edged horizon. On its peak, lost in the clouds, generations of stag hunters wander for centuries. Glistening of the setting sun. All the signs say: end of Indian summer. If I hear it right, nothing comes from your lips. Are you dumb? Blind? Perhaps you're searching through memory for the shapes of all prints—footsteps in the snow, old songs and cognac in the evening, small white towns with castles and turrets, the smells of Sunday afternoons, the river running under granite bridges. As if this, too, escapes you. Here, under the empty sky of ancient tribes you never heard about, you'll end your way. I, of course, always return. You don't. Which makes all the difference.

The sodden moss sinks underfoot when we cross half-frozen bays and walk through birch groves, wandering in an uneven circle that widens into darkness, through the minds and bodies of men and animals trapped in last year's snow—no: trapped from the beginning, emptiness all around us, ice collecting on our pale faces, I can hear you singing on the run, an unknown melody, I can't make out the words, clouds of breath freeze on your fur collar, eyes open wide as we trudge through silence and weakening starlight, through the fevered babble of children exiled to distant camps, insects curling up under bark, December or June, no difference, ashes blanket the ground as far as you can see, damp wool of shirts, we wade through the fog rolling in from the hills, oozing into our lungs, hills where there must be flowers about to bloom under a woman's eyelids, who dreams of dark faces hardening into granite, the snow's covering us, we're asleep on our feet, under the steel-gray sky, oblivious to the rhythms of sunrise and sunset, endless, as if they never began, our teeth crack in the cold, we don't want to separate, I can barely swallow, tell me the lyrics of your song, I want to sing with you.

The East Coast lies behind you, pulsing mind, nests of dead birds in which the hardening shells of eggs—stronger than fire and ice—smother the androgynous embryos, you wade through marshes, suffocating fogs and villages of hundred-year-old sages who no longer recognize their gods— their ancestors appearing in nightmares that overwhelm the patient ones living in anonymity, you, strong and calm, journey farther, through endless pine forests, where herds of deer with poisoned blood boiling in their veins stampede toward the vast lakes of the Far North—only to find death in the spears of small, quick hunters, who months earlier rowed out from the frozen spot stitching the continents together, smoothly, without resistance, you slip through the silk curtains of mist, which spread like a dark fleet sailing across the sea, leaving a wake of foam—closing in an instant, along the infinite rivers where the bellies of killed fish glisten, you journey through gorges and canyons, up riverbeds of minerals to the heart of the sacred mountain, a dark place in the middle, glowing silently, a steady force, you breathe on it, touch it, softly, in a scream from the deep—rupturing your eardrum—you hear the moans of your star-crossed companions overcome by eternal sleep, a rock face smoothed by kisses reflects your innocent eyes aglow with sweet pain, the pelvic bones spread, splashing you with salty juices, a volcanic eruption instantly hardening into a shield.

Horses sculpted in black marble. In town squares swept by gusts of winter wind. Rip themselves off their pedestals? No: perhaps they're tempted to go with the boy. The one who woke this morning, serious and dizzy. Woke from sleep overrun by a faint image, blurring. His companions try to keep him from leaving right away. He walks in silence toward the North. Across wheat fields, through birch groves. He won't rest till he reaches the glacier. While he ages like wine. Will he return? Eskimos lead him safely through snowfields and over the Bering Strait, in their boats he sleeps easily. Like anyone would: this is his home. Not that he would erase memory. Only in the glint of frozen water, in crystals and smooth ice does day become bitter enough for him. Only one step—and what was once solid disappears. In the dreams of other men the boy looks calmly over the dark backs of horses and knows what I don't know how to say. Others would need a lifetime. Today, tomorrow, yesterday: it's all the same. I, too, will do what I should have done long ago.

Now, in a bitter or a soft voice, in the lengthened melodies of a lament, in flooding and cracked mirrors, brute force of soldiers and the blind offspring of nomadic animals disturb your sense of reality, which changes like shifting archipelagos in the South Seas, now, in lush cascades of corn, flowing toward a sewer like the pale blood of mortally-wounded dolphins, in moments of horror, before you sink into sleep, which won't release you from the memory of exile, now, when you say snow and everything remains the same, in a sad song, slyly imitating the rhythm of a long run across infinity, now, hopelessly, passionately, hastily here, the door ajar, through which water leaks, now, when the walls are closing in and snail shells crack underfoot, now, in the ripe clusters of hail nailing you to the ground, now, at the end and beginning of paths closing, now, in the dark voice coming from the night you shared with everyone lost like you; do you recognize yourself in this poem?

In this moment, in the twilight of a cold room, thunder approaches from a distance, through storm windows and dusty panes, in late afternoon, the water in the pot doesn't boil, when fish gasp under the ice, when half-asleep you tremble, as if without hope, when a pack—a herd of shivering stags leaves the dried marshes deep in the woods and comes to the gardens in town, this fleeting instant, when the cold slices through your spine, when hardened honey cracks in jars, when the thought of a woman's hand—laid on the forehead of the dying—comes closer and closer, when from the depths of memory destroyed villages you wanted to forget begin to rise, when guilt and truth burn your stomach, when frightened pheasants are flushed from tapestries hanging on the wall, when guards leaving their posts whistle to one another, piercing the air, when a sharp stone breaks your skull, should I remind you now that your wounded body will be no different than the shadow a solitary bush casts across the trampled earth, east of Eden?

A River and a Young Woman

We sit in the shadows of the monastery wall—or what's left of it, the next westbound bus due in half an hour, tears gathering in your eyes—or maybe it just seems that way, I see you crying at the swimming pool, when you were six, washing chlorine from your eyes, how in beautiful abandon your lips and breasts swell, how you sing in a bold voice, in the orange grove whose entrance has been closed to foreigners for decades, thousands and thousands of miles away, on another continent, how you pout when you can't say what you want, like me now, when for the first time I realize I'm not with you, not under the same sky, in the distance the resting workers murmur in Spanish, you shiver, no longer thinking of burning deserts and dream landscapes, places you want to visit before straying too far to return, I lean close to hear what's on your mind: no, I don't know who owns the world—if that's what you're asking, all the other unnecessary encounters disappear from this sequence, your face blurs: my loneliness is the same as yours.

The light in the poem I know by heart spreads over the hills. I'd rather be there, of course. But here, in front of me: a sleeping figure. I don't know who it is. I can only guess: someone who finished a story begun long ago. Someone who knows the difference between speech and silence. Without despair, guilt, glory, hatred. I know his desires, his needs are behind him. He sleeps, but not forever. Fast and sure as the dusk settling on the girl's head, when she hurries home through the cornfields.

You write about another time. Like me. Sometimes even better. About men. Women. Memories, which weaken by the hour. About the uneasiness of strangers meeting in visions. Damp darkness over the Alps, in rooms. It's drizzling. Someone we know sets out for Berlin. Cold stars twinkle. We've been locked up for less than half a century, each in his own speech, although we share the same world, the same torments. Does it hurt you as much as it hurts me? Daybreak: what more can I tell you?

For a friend in Zagreb

A backwoodsman—or maybe only a tight-lipped peasant from the hills bordering an almost inaccessible Alpine village, ancient, I imagine: dejected, but not resigned. The last in his family who can speak to stags, he journeys from his harsh climate, through high and low tides, to a remote village at the northern tip of a Pacific island, the name escapes me, unmapped, lost in the hum of insects, in the labyrinth of overgrown paths and clearings turning back into rain forest, to meet a woman who understands the dialects of fish. At the village entrance, near a loose circle of huts, he sees her wave to him, excited, opening her mouth: no sound. He winces, stops, neck dripping, sweat running down his chest. He stands still: language can't compete with silence. The buzzing midges around his head reveal eternity—the days he spent in front of his house, on the doorstep, up in the hills.

After all, why sadness? Why fear? We don't know the depths of Finnish lakes, the cold of the Siberian taiga, the map of the Gobi desert. We don't even know what's in your dreams. Mine, too. That's the way it is. But you, as always: listening in the dark, lighting matches, gazing straight ahead. The man whose name you won't forget—even in the middle of the night—still hasn't called. You're hungry. In the corner of the room an old man in a rocking chair creaks back and forth, the shining keys of the sax laid on its side reflect your soft face, which you hide from yourself and others. Framed by the window, horses hover above the ground, wandering aimlessly through men's destinies, silk tails sailing in the wind. And for a moment, while the old man leans over a book—leafed through hundreds of times—you see the riders galloping across the fields, through the woods, heads down, black hair waving in the setting sun, the vanishing sun. Gone. Is that why you can't remember the short poem describing the whole world as it was and will be, why dusk blinds you to the stories of everyone, stories known only to the man whose name you won't forget—even in the middle of the night, the man who stands somewhere in the open, alone, in the dark, on the high plains?

Ways of Saying Goodbye

So winter approaches, she tells herself. Not quite yet, not really, but soon, if I may add. She stares into a river the color of dark olives. Higher up, at the source, it flooded its banks, flooded villages, drowning people and animals. Now it flows calmly. As if nothing happened. The woman I'm describing lies on the hillside: warm ground, a carpet of wildflowers. Her wound sears her. Sometimes she rises absently, and gazes eastward into the distance, and sings sotto voce, splitting the trunks of pines, softening the shuddering hides of deer. She knows no medicine will cure her hope. Above the surface of the water insects, half-frozen, swarm. Only when the wind gusts through the reeds and cloud-packed sky does she wince and for a moment recognize her fear—the way her heart beats only as hard as mine. Only.

On the south side of Malta, where steep cliffs fall into the sea, near stone towers I'm sure men didn't build, there's a garden, unfenced, almost hidden in thick grass, full of sweet-smelling bushes and fine dust settling on his sneakers. In the corner of the garden, where he will never walk again (neither alone nor with the woman who was with him then), a small lake appears, perhaps only a puddle that won't dry. And doesn't reflect his image. It's not important now. I want to say: the plant stems flow with sap, the earth suffers quietly, in the twilight tired eyes rest, sounds fade before the ear can make them out, a storm's brewing, the air vibrates as in the dreams of great painters, the wound continues to burn, swarms of bees buzz above the waves of the sea. I'm afraid the past, the people he lost, can't be translated into sentences with verbs, nor can I summon them back into living memory. I believe that. That's how it happened.

The port grows dark. Across the bay, inmates in the island prison stroke their sweaty bellies. Rain washes the streets, as if before an earthquake. Somewhere two hands clap steadily till morning. In the bus station a boy and a girl have their picture taken. While he stays still. Absent. Mumbling the names of those he loves. In fevered sleep the man next to him turns over on his side, almost raises his head, as if the names he'll never learn to pronounce have stolen into his leaden dreams, and then he sinks back under his blanket. The dull ache in his chest doesn't stop. In the room: perfect peace, aging wooden beams. He tries to cry. Fails. In the bakeries the Chinese start to work.

San Francisco, October 1986

The last thing I remember may be the smell of burnt bread. Now I think it's clear: we'll never end this conversation. I'm leaving. We'll meet again in a few hours, maybe in a few years. Look: a warm handshake, dry palms, thoughtful gaze, no fear, long farewell. I'm leaving you by the unread newspapers. No hard feelings, no sadness. Pigeons coo in the deserted houses on the hill. Everything's as it should be. Through the window boats sail toward the horizon. Damp, heavy air. Sour grass rustling in the corner of the garden. Do you, too, believe I'm walking farther and farther, almost going on a journey? Maybe even to Alaska? Who knows?

At daybreak, as we journeyed through the emerging light, I imagined midwestern prairies covered with snow, empty village squares, buildings without tenants, towns like dying wolves bleeding from slashed bellies, helpless, behind me. On front lawns tattered flags wrapped around flagpoles, brown leaves rotting in the wind, I wonder if the birds were awake at all, sleeping day and night, as if the strong gusts scattering pages of yesterday's newspapers across the squares didn't suit their smooth feathers, too cold for their hollow bones. In thick bushes I wanted to see the gleaming eyes of wild hounds, dense swarms of flies quivering above bare trees, cool reflections in the ponds of freezing frogs, the faces of loved ones lost in time, mothers suckling their babies in the anxiety of morning, packed trains from the suburban ghettos, old men who faint from heavy smells, tears on the cheeks of a blind boy. And I know: the convoy hasn't reached the maternity hospital yet, workers light their first cigarettes in the moment between night and day, no one belongs to anyone, names, dreams, skies filled with stars disappearing.

The river rushes on. As it has for a long time. Herons, or wading birds that look like the herons in field guides, are getting ready to fly south. Reeds rustle in the evening wind, in the breeze off the water. Here and there. The houses lining the bank fade in mist. Pale light fills the windows. Seated by the lamps, people dream of soldiers entering their lives. Sweet apples in their cellars: if no one eats them, they'll begin to rot. A thirteen-year-old girl keeps practicing piano sonatas. Stiff fingers. Steady wind. Hours running on. In everyone's eyes: growing boredom. Think twice. You can also bid farewell. After all, you'll only be changing ways of saying goodbye. I was just like you long ago.

Empty Rooms

Things can't go on like this forever, no words, no shapes, a smeared watercolor. Perhaps it's not too late: somewhere water still spills over the edge of the fountain, somewhere an answer may be found. Let's say a dark flock of sparrows still plays in the yard, a scream returns as an echo, dreams—if they are dreams—never change their meaning, river boats still float with the current. Perhaps it's not too late. That's how I know you can't tell me anything I don't already know. I know I exist. For instance: is this not my own high-pitched voice winding up through the stairways? Is this not my own palm? But why such pain, hope, fear? At once I recognize my own self. Yes, that's me. No doubt about it. That's me.

It could even be a church. Without portals, frescoes, stucco. Smoothly sculpted in brittle stone. Perhaps. As if hauled from a distance, from the unknown into hot desert sand. In this space: I remain as I was. You're the one who changes. The passing hours slowly carry you through February. You're sitting, perhaps all afternoon, under the arches I'm certain a madman dreamed up. The warm sun works its way through the cracks in the ceiling. Specks of light, a whole web glistening on black canvases. I don't know if you can tell the shadows from the wall. Holding your breath. Utterly still. The outlines of the faces you met and forgot, your brothers and sisters, the Russian steppe you traveled over so many times, all blur together, all disappear. Calm fills the air, as if in the mountains. Perhaps muffled voices, even humming—it's true—coming from somewhere. Empty echoes. Sinking into you. Softening you until you're completely changed. Alive to passion. Longing. The chirping of a titmouse. How you paired off to walk across the Karst high meadows to the sea. (In a way you're still walking.) That whisper, I can't tell what it is: singing dervishes from Konya? A half-finished poem by a Romanian, who will die far from the shores of the Danube, filled with nostalgia? Besides, what interests me is you—sinking into dusk. Your face buried in your hands. You see nothing. Your eyes will open only when day comes to an end. And you'll be older, years older, though the monks living here would tell you only a moment has passed. You'll be old enough to recognize a thing or two: a love that lasts longer than any separation.

Rothko Chapel
Houston, February 1988

The guts of the cuttlefish water down its ink. Birdcall in low clouds. Probably a windhover. The sunbaked blocks of stone begin to cool. Summer thaws. Sweet smell of a cicada's broken wing. And you—where are you in this vision? Do you stare through waves of reeds? If it's really you, then you aren't talking to the man by your side. Leaning forward, as if in the middle of a field, he wants to know what catches your eye. Focused on the horizon. Glistening in the dark, as if before a storm. No worse than the shadows trembling on the walls of your room, the horrifying portraits of a stranger drawn by twilight. This moment won't pass. Ever. A boy runs over sand dunes. Does he know language offers many words for the same thing?

The image—lost forever—comes to life again. Always the same room, embedded in darkness. Flies on the cracked walls. In the stale air, the smell of stomach acids and urine. A child immersed in a picture book of exotic plants, frozen in an endless moment. A blue labyrinth of veins shines through his white skin. Was he raised in love by Albanian women in the damp and dark? A face bitterness turned pale. Dry pears on the windowsill. Still life. The sand in the hourglass turns into dust. Someday, somewhere, perhaps this boy, now at rest, will become a man who travels, cries, causes pain. Who will think of home only when he catches a reflection of eyes—as lonely as ours—staring back at him from mirrors, sand, and grass. Doubts will ravage him. Visions of abandoned ports, pride, drunkenness—everything will haunt him.

The dripping tap. Keepsakes in the drawer. Glowing coals. The cat's nest on a friend's bed. The sky comes down. Fruit rots in the grass. Bruised by September. Abstracted, you stroll down the back streets, through the coastal village. The port drifts off to sleep, moaning in terror. In bare feet you feel the earth, every stone, every plant. Time, unspent, hardens in the bronze bells of the cathedral. Another strange sound, like the sigh of a sick child in early evening, vanishes into nothingness, into history. Are you coming? Going? Your hand's half-raised to greet or wave goodbye, like this:

In this humidity, mosquitoes swarming above the cotton fields that must sprawl beyond the levees, I lean against an ancient pillar, imagining on this porch a woman who longed for Paris, halfway to the noisy port, to the delta where ships from the East no longer anchor, the babble of young travelers, I turn my back on them with ease, memory leaves me only a snatch of the blues the blind black man sang yesterday in a bar, the smell of the palm trees in a garden hidden from the house I'm staying in comforts me. So now I think of you, serious boy, troubled friend, name fading on a gravestone. How you wrote of flowers changing shape when sadness overcomes them. Of taxi drivers, places you didn't visit, love untouched by time—and those who understand that: like you and me.

New Orleans, December 1988

[FROM] THE CITY AND THE CHILD

for both of you

Grand Hotel Europa

Faces in Front of the Wall

Humble is the charity of early mornings. Everything that happens then
must happen: to you, to me, to the whole world. Temptation
is great indeed: we gaze, enchanted, as a fire's eternal glow
melts the columns of cathedrals, a virgin's slumber, and the hidden

spring of a toy. We watch, motionless, as in a tranquil family crypt.
Each of us, I think, is already doomed. We're silent. What else could we do?
Like a stunned witness in a country when it was still
a country. It lives on, exiled into an image which won't let us sleep.

Day and night quiver in our pupils. Do we kneel, hoping the storm will take
pity on us and bring a mother's gentle forgiveness? That it will blur the line
between the altar and the offering? I guess, I know:

There's no greater mistake. Embers cover the fire screen. Even the blood
spilling down a girl's hip has lost its taste. It doesn't smell like plowed soil
crumbling in our fingers. In vain we try: we're less than a footnote.

Weather Forecast

A spring shower rushes over the sunken monarchy. Will it ever end?
The rhythm striking the window lulls me into a deep coma.
I hand myself over to silence and flow into damp soil
so that in a year or two I can live in a cloud: my true sanctuary.

A faithful horse takes a Cossack toward town. Perhaps the rider
doesn't know it yet: his death, like all languages erased from the earth,
will be laid at invisible feet. Even greater adventurers await the end
of the natural cycle. But it's not up to me to judge.

I can only rain on the crying child in diapers, on carts
and burnt skyscrapers, on the tobacco smuggling route. I rain:
I don't ask where the widows in black have gone. I cover everything,

like a transparent varnish. I rain. On a balance, on coffins
used for shelter. I rain down on the spine of the boy who will stand
before a line of sturdy soldiers, give an order, and the line will shudder.

Grand Hotel Europa

The carline thistles wither in the vase on the shelf. No man's land
beckons me. I'm guilty because I won't forget. That would be easy
like the course of a hasty flock cutting the sky. I lean against the window,
as others have before me. The taste of fruit, the nude woman

who visits me in dreams: nothing I touch surprises me anymore.
And the harmony of a still life doesn't help. A different pain
blinds me. I want to share it with someone. But with whom? If I
whisper it alone into the night, its echo won't find its way back. If

we all speak it vanishes, like a copper engraving in a blast furnace.
But I cannot renounce it. Mine is the fear of the fugitive who couldn't hide
in this cheap room. When the merciless god covers the window frame only

the mirror will preserve their faces. I'll lend them my throat to intercept
the barking of dogs and the blare of a hunter's horn. I can't even see myself
anymore, yet I must sing for them to find peace in my song, finally united.

Grapes of Mercy

Come back to lighten our soul and let the contagious steam
evaporate in the extra verse. Come back to spin the axis,
to weight and center bedrooms again. Here, where the union
of animals and clay depends on a weak hunch, here you mean more

than water to a captive muttering the Pater Noster. Come back
to guide our hands with the allure of fruit we don't dare pick.
Without you we cannot distinguish between the seasons, we can
only make wild guesses. The neck is rigid, and storks are flying south.

It's high time: come. Present us with a gift, the key to the future,
to noble nostalgia. It's enough that you exist. Like a fragrance
which doesn't go up in smoke when our first woman leaves us. Solitude

must move you to test us in perfection. Let us be in pain. You'll be with us
like a stain spreading over a clay jar: first a small spot, then a flood
softening the edges until the room gives way under its own weight.

Pastoral

The ornament of frost and jasmine is already crumbling. Before
a tent, a thrush generously scatters psalms across the earth. The day
is almost gone. I have mercy for the future scar, like a letter
in which a private Iliad begins. A kiss on the forehead—

I give it lightly: a father moans on his deathbed, the family
has left. One is missing, inspiring black epics. For a long time
he has been marching elsewhere. He surrendered to the spell
of the banner fluttering above the castle. I had wished

that at least the youngest lamb would see the zenith.
But the forms of darkness are everywhere. What could I have done?
I left home like a pilgrim bound for Rome. I departed early.

Had I not gone, my lost brother would not have lifted a hand against me
in a nomadic hallucination. Thus the road is marked with mines and I can
only stutter. No symmetry, no design: an ancient seal cracks imperceptibly.

Mercenaries

The wind has died down in the vineyards on the hills. A moth flaps
against a carbon lamp. Evening draws a feeble breath. A prayer, unheeded,
disappears in the twilight. God remains indifferent. From a distance
we watch the heirs to a mighty throne tremble at the decrees. Dynasties

endlessly rise and fall. North and south, east and west: we serve you
faithfully. The triumphal arch pierces the clouds. It's not mulberry juice
that sticks to our palms. We grip our shields. In a dismembered country
a tangled vine grows in neglect. We can only guess at its suffering. Langobards,

Scythians, masters of Norik: in the name of another's victory we opened
treasuries and skulls, leaving behind us empty caverns. Now we rest.
Our work is done. It won't be easy to begin again.

Our sight, too, has given out. All we can see is the simple order
of things. Not much, less than nothing. We don't even recognize
the face in the puddle when at times it reflects our own image.

Migrations

Cosmopolis

Listen well: is that the trumpet call? The cavalry
rides through history. The shadow of an ancient battle
wants to be the truth again. A distant stairway winds toward a cloud.
Mountains fall, a chalice trembles. Emptiness spills over

the edge. Yet you, miraculously, grow faster than you can be
destroyed. A titmouse will not leave its nest. The west wind
tempts you with redemption in a hollowed loaf of bread
at the Last Supper. A broken toy. More children are missing.

Yet you endure. You interrupt the world's monologue, its endless drone.
You're the flickering snow on the screen, which is always on. The vault
of the universe above you is crystal clear. The rest of us

stare helplessly into the cold prison of the stars. We watch a finger
rise from the flame flickering behind your back, which never consumes you.
And on the arch of the sky the finger writes, tirelessly, "I am."

for Josip Osti
Sarajevo-Ljubljana

Migrations

You see everything, everything: the breath of flies, a teapot
whistling, a cartridge recklessly shot off at daybreak, a pattern
on the wallpaper, the gloom of a concert hall, dusty violins left
in haste on the floor, an inscription in the language of the two

prophets who came to the Slavs, things drowning in infinite
light, a scream tearing suddenly across the sky, gleaming metal,
a column of children and women carrying newborn babies, the scent
of basil in a garden, a trickle of plum juice oozing into the rutted

tracks left by retreating armies. Everything. You see graveyards.
And metastases of white-hot pyres. Here the world we know lets out
its final gasp. The ancient order of violence is returning to the hearths.

The magic of words is dying out. And a girls' choir stands in silence.
A trail points east, across a snowy pass. Nothing erases it.
Now you know the bell tolls for you and for us.

The City and the Child

No cry, really, is meaningless. Only when an archangel
appears, like a blue gentian on a mountain slope, do we know,
if only for an instant, our native land. Your Babylonian
moan won't die away. That's why poets never sleep. The task

seems clear now: this will be a chronicle of pain.
The size of a melting glacier. Which floods poppy fields
and villages, targets painted on the portal's slender frieze,
the lush filigree of Turkish silver: each tear deepens you.

You stand on the immovable rock. The world around you crumbles
into the abyss. You drink the water of life, drawn from the mouths
of those who breathe with you. Each morning they come to witness

your rebirth. Like this poem. It won't be long before an avalanche
silences it. But a thousand echoes will spring up in its place. For the love
flowing through your veins is the seed, the blossom, and the fruit.

Metamorphosis of Grass

(on a theme by Ovid)

The grass on a grave grows faster than memory. A green down blanket
hides ankles and palms. And the sapling of guilt planted in the liver
grows like the choir's silence when the cantata ends. It's true:
when this song is over no one will live in its verses.

Longing weighs on me when I open doors. I go from room to room
and across the hills of Galilee, which sense the coming drought.
I confess: I sing sotto voce. The radio drowns me out. Yet something
orders me not to renounce the word. The word which will outlive

this generation. Sharper than salt oozing through the walls
of the heart. I stumble down the overgrown path. If I have to,
I'll take into my arms the animal whimpering in the brambles.

Over lilies I go, past the last man. Through the crudest months
I wade alone. Not just April: eternity separates me from my brother.
And in the house the carpet turns to hair, like a meadow.

The Imperfect Passion of a Word

Where a flock of starlings should fly—only the emptiness
of air breaks open. Barrels of oil have been burning for a long time.
Hardly an image of paradise, it's true. But not yet hell. Old men
sing lamentations under the ruins of the brick arcades. It's enough

that one solitary child listens to them from a foreign land. The echo
of a ballad gives him strength. Heavy, dark birds glide through
sleep, and in their unbridled lust boys discover light. A razor blade
slices across a young face and tenderness now seems heroic. They say

a draft of a sonnet can't be squeezed out of memory's decay.
Well, perhaps. But that would be a bitter image. I can only say:
silence interests me less than the imperfect passion of a word,

from which a seed explodes into flower. Channeling the delirious
vows of strangers, the century's bodies and souls, into the aqueduct
of language: I know in my blood that this is not in vain.

The Beauty of Failure

A shimmering comet burns out above the woods and water.
Karst wine ages in noble barrels. You love the sweet torment
of song. You are drawn to a place where you can name
everything. And here the century turns: language

takes no shortcuts. You, who easily revive the sleep
of the unborn, waited, in vain, in a hotel room for the majestic
deer to approach as they did in the past, when you hunted freely,
naked and strong, over the plains of many kingdoms.

You follow morning's first frightening light, which instantly
sobers drunks and changes you into a seer. And yet you doubt
your gift. You did not feel the hush laid across the fur

of deer gathering in herds. Which out of loyalty to you renounced
caves and dens. Which long awaited your turning from hunter
to shepherd so that the Milky Way would once again appear.

for Tomaž Šalamun
at home and abroad

Young Muse

Young Muse

My ears, no, more precisely, my capillaries and body are tuned
to your cry. Gazing at an archipelago of stains on the wall,
I marvel, like Leonardo: how wide is the horizon! Bending over you,
I deliver myself to the fate pronounced by a newborn's sigh.

And a star blissfully touches me. I can't describe how tenderly
you punish me with sleepless nights, with the laurel wreath's sweet torment.
This ritual: intoxicatingly beautiful but wordless. Though I don't exist
outside verse, even I fall silent for a moment to make room for the miracle

of this day. May it never end. What was separate before you arrived
now breathes together, like a nest of quail. Fluttering fills the sky,
which isn't sinless. Yet I know: there's only one festival. I celebrate it

when you wake. The muse who removes the shadow from your cheek
comforts me, like a messenger worn down by generations. And she whispers
the name, a new source, which opens the doors to the houses of strangers.

Boundless Room

Yes, I belong to those who were once under the spell
of blood. And wild animals leaping from Utopian scenes
into life to leave a mark on the hunter. And people
shaped by the age of crime and restless sleep.

I'm not saying the roar of the underground river I used
to sail attracts me anymore. I'm not saying that at all.
But the wound which condemned me to lordly solitude
has changed form. Once I was one, now I'm a tribe.

And the anguish of a boat setting off from shore inspires me
only in a mirror. I see myself only in the trembling
of a small body conjured by the sweet confusion of my desire.

I humbly praise this joy: how you show me where to receive
the gift of manna. I serve your breath redolent of milk.
I don't sleep at night so day will shine more truly.

Church Bells at Midnight

You wake up. In your own time. Like a dull red aster.
Which blooms at night, when no one's watching. Duty
and the aroma of coffee beckon me. Though I have
traversed the smooth sides of glaciers, crossed oceans,

and tied the continents together, this window is now the final
frontier. With a cautious caress I uncover your body, which glows
like silver when you turn to me. And the weight of my delight
commands me to sober up. To shed my habits. To dictate,

in a simple way, my last will and testament: for you the world will be
an open hand. No cold drafts. Memory's embers smolder forever
in a fishpond. It is you now, not me, who eagerly awaits

the new moon. And the force and subtlety of the only name I whisper
in your ear. Don't say it. Heed the footprints of sleepwalkers
while the chaos lasts. Then measure the shadow and the sky.

Gratitude

The arc of your eyebrows—so new!—draws a splendid dome
in the air. Supported by the down of the angels, the ones who guard
the doors to language. Its only rival is the grace of the silent ballerina.
Imperfect verbs: like the green snow you see now for the first time.

How it lies on a mountain range you cross in an instant. Like a comet
carrying a spark from one body to another. Your little arms embrace
the whole planet. You question the secrets of the full moon. You are
a stranger to passers-by, a gift to me: from the touch of two languages

your will grows. You take in everything, like a viaduct
boldly stretching from mother to daughter. You make
agnostics see: the sky, that quilt of lightning, is more beautiful

than a field of buckwheat. Even I'm struck. You were washed clean
when you revealed yourself to me: the eternal word. I'll admit:
I'm grateful to you for guiding me safely through the throes of birth.

Invocation by a Small Bed

The water bubbles in the radiator. And the ebb and flow of the sea
were recorded in the annals. At noon, I was absolved by the horizon.
I sense my journey is not complete. I'm just faithfully preparing
for the next task, like any father. Perhaps I'll make mistakes.

Yet the delight of discovery is sweeter than the taste
of summer's first strawberry melting on my tongue. I watch
like a treasure hunter: from your forehead I brush away the lock
of hair that upset your sisters around the world. I want more!

I want to be a crystal goblet humming under your gaze!
More disciplined than a Jesuit, I want to yearn like the gentle
breath that multiplied the wheat in our ancestral granaries.

Free of spells and doubts until my body lets me down, I want
to be like balm mint at dawn. I learn kinship's vital ties by heart.
I'm untouchable. And thrilled to learn there is no other way.

Newborn Ode

A soft baritone lifts you up, the one that drives the sap
through the neighbor's cherry tree! The lunar eclipse that covered
your forehead glorifies you! And in the cupboard a porcelain
bowl vibrates softly, like an alto sax! Cinnamon

is honored to be compared to the fragrance of your hair! When the vein
in your wrist pulses the beginning and the end of time dissolve
into a hymn of marble slabs! You grow faster than a river changing course
under bridges. You rise miraculously, like yeastless bread. When I glide

my hand over your body, smaller than a ripe fig, the sky glows.
Like fireworks. I touch the soft crown of your head, which throws
the compass needle into confusion. It opens for clarity—no longer accessible

to me. But it pours infinitely into you as from a fragile jug. Your breath
drives me to the edge. Sometimes it makes me dizzy. Yet I stand firm.
When I hold you in my arms I'm the rock from the Old Testament.

UNENDED

for you, almost unconditionally

The Promise

I don't look over my shoulder, no idea
where I'm headed and not an ounce of fear,
falling like fluff from an eiderdown quilt,
sinking in the afternoon air, real as an hour
of solitude or the fragrance of an herb.
My wounds are healed over and all five senses
in sync, harmonized to the birds and the sky,
the grimy wall of an underpass with graffiti
scratched in a child's hand, announcing
I was here. But not only here, my lord, as you
know, I go where you want me to be—
tonight, for instance, I am a wave
you push across the Old Square, underground
through a parking garage, over the banks
of a lazy green river and over the files
on a drawing desk of another architect.
Come, a whisper says, and again
I flood the channel, at one with
the darkened air above the city and the steppe,
like the pillow you smooth and soften up
for someone unable to sleep,
lying along the world as it slowly goes out.

Drowned Love

You burn me, this is my weakness.
I admit: I can't stand that everything
—words and bodies—passes
from hand to hand. Like a walk
down to the three bridges, past bookstores
and the ornaments almost invisible
on each façade, past the stains
on violins, shiny and hard
like madness, past the palaces
in no hurry to be restored,
an orchestra playing day after day
in another gazebo, another park,
when I lost my way among the streets
and wandered, ignorant, under the dome
of another sky, in another dream,
which threatens and seduces
just like you, who lure
a trout to your hips, who foretell
how memories twist in the genes.
You burn me, this is my weakness.
Like an omen I can't dismiss.
From a hand to another hand. Tears,
I know this too well, tears
don't run down the cheeks,
they're oil a downpour can't wash off
and high tide breaks against the soul
in vain. There's nothing else I can do:
I give you up to the current,

and I do it out of love. You vanish
into pain, a strange joy, and nothing.

Hymn to the Favorite City

The ground is soaked with weeks of high water,
and thieves of sanctuaries beside the lagoon
are on the run, my eyes follow them.
Somewhere close, a robin's breast collapses
under the pressure of a thumb: only a little while
before the dock a slender boat leans against
is covered with drops of blood, useless
as a song two people can hardly hear.
Maybe it's merely a melody.
This city has baptized a dozen generations
in the sacrament of war, but I go on
all the same. I don't have a choice.
The harlequin from the Palazzo Grassi,
the one who inspired Picasso, has meaning for me
only when I see you rendered blue,
faint and luxurious, with the violence
beauty uses to enter certain homes:
indivisible, unable to end, like a cloud
that houses thunder, beneath which I work
my memories and widen channels
and clear out passageways, so the voice
that surges out of you can spill downstairs
to the living room, and cross the yard
in a rush basket I can barely see.
Carried by the echo through whirlpools
and across the shores of death, it says: no.

The Kiss

How it rises out of waves in the bay
and shudders like a gentle thrust
of the sea, which sooner forgives
than punishes, doomed as it is to feckless birth.
How it wakes me up, takes me inside
with a slender hand, with shimmering dust,
gliding like a guess or premonition, up and up
to the eyelashes, the eyebrows, the mouth,
and spilling across the face and over the ears,
where the cries of gulls are caught.
A hymn to the moment that lasts
and lasts, so nothing belonging together
will separate, like a boat that worries only about
its arrival in the harbor, dropping its anchor
next to a dock, so the story will reach
the close it was meant to reach. And the sailor,
once turned to a pillar of salt, will forever remain
doubled over, where lobes of water
linger like wedding guests
years after the flood has folded back.

Metamorphosis of Pain

A wall, covered with reddish ivy
that survived the winter, and over there
a glance the length of the empty street
and a man who might get old—
I say might, because new skin
never fails to cover a cut,
it tingles once in a while
more gently than a mistral
blowing through the rooms.
This much we know. All the same:
in the folds of the couch there's a book
and the sky, crushed into flocks
of birds and signs, scattered randomly
like islands in the Adriatic
or letters of poets lying open,
boys upheld by illusions of chewing
green, narcotic leaves from here
to hereafter—I among them.
I give the image, hardened in my spit,
a hundred names for god. I stand before it
like this, trembling like fingers parting curtains,
seeking comfort and a rush in my veins,
a creek in the distant hills
where everyone I know wants to end up.
Murmur of water, wellspring noise,
watering us as it waters me,
the meadow, the house, the grass,
the snow. Its sound makes a boy thirsty,
lost as he is in the landscape

of someone else's yard. His only hope
is that those who manage to stay alive
are a little holy and no less mad.

Simple Gift on the Hill

To you I give a tremor and the spinal cord
it afflicts, a peeled-off cone and white fibers,
slogans about the tendons and growing taut.
You forget nothing, will lose nothing. You must
store it all up. A task you did not choose.
May the tremor, then, gain force, until the brain
gets dizzy and the eyes, the eyes a blur of light:
there is no such thing as perfection.
How could there be, when the bay before me
wheezes under the weight of a tanker spill,
crude oil and feathers, the sadness of mothers
saying goodbye to their grownup sons
bound for every corner of the empire.
Sons who, like you and me, have not
allowed the blood in their veins
to thicken under seductions of routine.
How could perfection not cause pain
when I am forced, day in, day out,
like a homestead about to collapse,
to ask myself what awaits and where
I'm going, when pebbles whirl
in dry riverbeds, when conquered cities
fall, when the century now behind us
smolders, and the body hesitates.
May the last temple, fortress, turret not disappear,
may silence be older than a seal of wax.
In this silence, I who nurse the hope,
I ask you, take this gift.
That nothing will be in vain.

Grass Psalm

Seekers after sources and rivers,
messengers of useless desires, traveling
merchants, a spider in its web:
they keep me company this early
evening hour, in the privacy of a groggy soul
who stands and smokes and three kids
sleeping upstairs. In a dream, my years
of devotion grind by, and an image unfolds
less real than I would want. Look at it:
translucent, not the least bit shy, it radiates
like an apparition over desert sands
others have discovered; but all the same it suits me,
so big and unsatisfied, like a monologue
running without a break, it lasts
as long as the pain of harvest grass
when left to rot. Look at me as I tremble,
you cannot miss how I reach for you,
my partner I do not know. Yet you alone
can fix my sight, you're a welcome
guest in every house, you detect
the failures in my speech, you forgive
the stutter that I am.

The Emigré Writer on the Dragon Bridge

An open suitcase, they used to say,
hides destinies unknown out here:
from hotel to the central station and farther,
through the many years of wind, the passengers
touch Orion above, looking for comfort
in rituals down here, in a sleepy countryside,
a consolation they no longer get
from photographs and books about
the lives their ancestors led. The everyday
favor could now be a prayer, a cup of herbal tea,
patience with endless explanations,
and a silent handshake when language will not obey,
like scattered coins, or a ceiling so low
it suffocates, big things putting fear
in little souls. From the south,
an alluring heat brings whiffs of memory,
for everyone, of course, is guiltiest
when love's at stake.
The one thing they still hunger for
rises without a sound from the waiting-rooms
and chairs too stiff for mercy,
and hangs, deceptively, like haze above
a fence which groans and splits beneath him
and allows him, for a second only, to rise—
why would he be an exception?—
before he vanishes in the river's waves
which swell against the banks and over,
taking with them the suitcases, carrying off

the books, toward a delta, a false reprieve,
a song that's poorly sung.

Ljubljana, summer 1994

To My Few Friends

Above the herd of white cities and above
the fires that frame them, a scarlet kite
appears for a moment, guided by a child's hand.
Come. Just follow me. It isn't far to where
you will have a view of ripened fruit
as it remains, lying in wet grass:
the order must have been fulfilled.
Unbearable, yet necessary, like the horizon
that dams the light and softens
the defeat of human shadow.
You too will lie, it's your habit.
Here you will count your handshakes
with the neighbors, errors in the language
and a horror of runaway troops, the biography
of castle walls, of streets and public squares,
saliva, heartbeat, sinew, semen,
some murals and portraits, forgettable
decrees. Come. Follow me. Here you will
shiver like I shiver, in labor and in love:
it is easy to live without memory, but not
without the legacy of what runs in the veins.
For now I pray apart, but I don't want
to kneel in private forever—come,
follow me, since no one would dare
to go there alone, in stammering
and drizzle, even for a little while,
evaporating out of the visible world.

The End of Homesickness

After every firefly has vanished into night
an emptiness remains. After
all the floods a polish sticks around.
Our faces don't recognize themselves
inside the worried reflection. Only a hill
disturbs us for a moment, moist and swelling
above the mattress edge: the slit of a skirt
that flashes open, rice falling opulent
on wings before the chosen couple's eyes,
and a young woman, who has not seen this
place before, waves her hand.
She invites us as if she had always been here,
resembling the dark green river
that laps against this castle and its fictitious
coat-of-arms, the garden with sandy paths
and a bedroom, where lovers from before
the war breathe in the curtains, waiting
for the stroll to finish, waiting with witnesses,
maids and mothers of tired families
waiting to go to bed, waiting to admire
two continents, waiting for the wrinkled
shirt, the high heels to come off.
The only one still awake,
I respond to the invitation, let myself
be drawn across the map: what used to live
as a single point is now becoming a line,
stronger from hour to hour and crossing
every border shaded by other hands.
Whispers, in your voice: Look, the country
is no longer such a huddled bird, it suffers
a little less than it did before.

Angels, Close Relatives

Homage to Marc Chagall

How there is neither anger nor bliss
on the faces of women, faces of men.
How the glow around their heads is sustained.
We accept it in slow surrender. Their destiny
pinches at the back of the neck. And how,
in their finest clothes, they fly above lost villages,
sift through flour sacks and through the hollow,
carmine sky, as the student of shadows
follows them, alone though not without trouble,
across the dunes, deserted streets, apartments
emptied in ancient ritual, so later he will know
the word for nothing, to comfort the witnesses who prove
how slight their bodies are, how they hover
within the canvas frame, beautiful and sad,
in grains of sand that sheen an hourglass,
how the wings of their coats rustle overhead
as the sand and glass are ground
beneath our feet, along our trail toward home
that doesn't change. Without them sensing
a rapture, or rancor, the freedom our faces feel,
features never given to simple sobbing—
as if tears had some lesson to teach.

Reclining on a Cushion

An early August morning that belongs to me,
like the mulberry that lives for the silkworm
forced to finish its commission
without haste, without mistrust.
I recognized you, don't worry.
Iodine and gold among the low hills
of a Sunday approaching noon
which resembles, suspiciously, the contours
of your body. A warm rain fuzzes every
inch of skin, or so I think, and takes responsibility
for a fertile harvest; desire asks
a single question of us all. Don't worry,
I recognized you. So it is pointless to answer,
as there is no point in poignant tremors
while I watch you sleep. Countries and cities
throb beneath your eyelids, the main square
filling up as I am filled with your moans,
and I am finally called by my own name:
it is enough for me to know
the road goes on without end.

Fidelity to the Sea

Liberation Street meanders uphill, I open
my nostrils wide, smelling Duino Castle
and the cliff face, lost in a land
that needs me as much as I need it, indifferent
to the book of hours and its rhythm
dictated to me years ago. Undying
smell of algae, the weight of dreams
made pure in the dark, the wild rose bush
and the deep sea, I leave them all behind
as I walk up. The fortress
like an animal, hibernating, hidden,
hidden from. Twilight of a stolen day
and look—there where the lens
won't reach, a pair of legs is spread,
dampness rejecting the difference between
a pitcher and a bowl. Look,
how far from the safety of form
I let the gaze be seduced, as if there is
no other way from the tower it's taken me
this long to conquer, but down into
the velvet glade where my exile began.
I descend feverishly, as though I might
miss out on something, as if this moment
I'm sinking into has been here
from the beginning, like a compass needle
faithful to the north.

Unanswered Plea

I learn things by myself, it's why
it takes so long. I ask for your patience.
It's not like I'm asking much.
I learn by myself, learn to cross the village.
It's not every day I recognize you
in the timberwork of the roof,
the builders' sweat still aglow in the air.
The river is sluggish here, the pond is asleep,
one's step less heavy, but I'm no longer
convinced I've read it right: these instructions
for painting a woodpecker's wings in red
and black and red, and how to cast a spell upon
the ankles of a pregnant girl. I don't know
nor want to know her name, and maybe that's
the reason I can't breathe. I won't forget
the way she makes me feel. Did I
read it right? Okay, I accept these signposts
in the humid moss, in the backbone curving
throughout every season, in scarlet shells
cracked apart at the feast to which I'm called.
I accept this. But where in the language
should I look for you, when language
is unworthy of what you are? It might be
that you assume a basic form, such as love,
or maybe you're something awful down the road
that will, come what may, come to pass.

In Her Footsteps

You walk by, slender as the season of sunlight
at the North Pole, men and women at a loss
for words, tears to nudge a heart follow the riverbeds
of history on their faces, even the palm tree
secretly swings to the rhythm of your stride,
even the ocean floor cannot stay still.
And here I stand and look, a barefoot boy,
a clear sky mistaken for a memory
of ancient times, when there was no horizon to see
and even the most attentive eye would find
no animal as sovereign as you when you walk by.
You walk by, the city is once again closing
behind your steps. All the way to the curbside
cherries have been washed up, the crowd
that follows you gathers them, and we admire you
together, this light is too intense for me alone.
Yet my knee bends in gratitude
when you neither ask nor offer anything, hinting instead
at the right to expect you, our one and only guest,
and you send us a signal, not wholly clear,
that though we change the images of your body
the law remains the same: this day must be blessed
in your name.

Without Saying

I claim the region of your belly,
joy rises within it like air in bread;
I lay along the line of night that breathes, heavy,
from your breasts across your hips, disappearing
into ever smaller circles of your navel,
which is closer to me than a wellspring
in my yard, I am more exposed than
a vulnerable slope, louder than a murmur in the ear
and nearer than the densely scattered stars.
It is quite possible I have a quarrel with laughter,
often, too, I am smashed to pieces, forgetting
my mother tongue, but there is one thing I feel:
my home is inside you, in the forests of this land
and its bakeries, white with heat;
I take pleasure in the crust and its warm center
where I leave behind secret marks.
So only the first, hesitant light outlines a calendar
of days that pass away, like a touch a bit unsure,
mindless of my open hand that wants to glide forever
over the roundness of your thighs.

Guardian of Solitaries

I keep forgetting, I forget, lean forward and reach
beneath myself, between the pages of a book
I read with one hand only, by heart I fumble
my way across the lines, toward the gate, through
hallucinations of young nuns who repeat the prayer
so there will be room for what is yet to happen:
for a moment, at least, I'm safe, though I must say
I shiver like a tiny bead of roe, which understands
that soon enough it will become a wave. All I really want
is a faithful manual for saying a private prayer,
courage amid the pattern of stains, beauty inside
a flashlight beam and unspent cartridges. A fidelity
dictated, after all, by someone who, standing
in the rose window of the belfry on that hill,
is, like me, obedient to another will, and caresses me
with a generous hand and lies on top of me, and every hour
expects the plea, the drying seed, to be answered.

Addict's Song

In the mirror across from our bed
the image of a paradise rises halfway
and the scent of island lavender
wakes up a thunder in the spine.
Unannounced and impossible to restrain,
its sound rips the arc of the body open
down the middle. To endure the rhythm
dictated by a dark silhouette of grace
and a blossom that smells sweetly
even when closed. To bear the happy ignorance
of whether you're a person or a narrow passageway
that sometimes withholds. To bear the whims
of a lost god, take penance upon myself:
this is the price to be paid, to endure and not
to leave the source, be bent as necessary,
and to drink, drink without stopping
from the honeycomb between your parted legs,
every moment spinning a promise of more.

In a Marseille Hotel Room

The key in my pocket doesn't keep me warm, I swear.
Darkness has been passing away for hours,
morning is almost here. I will never stop searching
for you. But I don't have a clue what has to be done.
The walls are warm and heavy scented, damp
from lonely visitors, their forgotten families.
I am going down the corridor, my fingertips
are trailing the wallpaper and the paintings
as I approach the destination and step
through the final door. I immerse myself
in the boiling white of clouds with no name,
tiny veins on the breasts, a map of muffled thrill.
Look, my lord, how it's not difficult at all
to choose a path. A choir in the pelvis starts singing,
the sky inflames when I plant the sapling,
it shoots up high, as fast as lightning, as nerves.
You scream, lord, and I with you:
warm milk pours across my face and floods me,
the city, the world. Foam and furrow show the way.
No hesitation. I follow you, I swear.

Eyewitness in the Garden

If it's true that people call to each other
from solitude to solitude, call one another in vain,
then here, in front of thousands of faces
fixed like statues staring blank and blunt,
I want to look, for the last time, at a flower:
a poppy as it waits for rain, perhaps,
a crocus or tulip refusing to bend,
or an iris that blooms three hours
before it fades—it doesn't matter.
I only want to make doubly sure
the world will be less than perfect
if you miss my being near. I just want
to take you in my hands, squeeze you
at the stem, weigh you and crush you
inside my fist, stagger and turn to liquid
and flow to where no place existed before.
In the air that inhales this fragrance
I want to breathe as long as there is breath,
to trickle through your hair and through
its roots, travel up the stiffened tube
all the way to the petals, at the top I want
to swear like a bead of water
the light shoots through, testify to the vertical
surge and make myself dizzy rising on my own.
The avalanche of blood in my fingers
takes away whatever power I had.
Forgive me if I'm a torrent of the past,
a memory that calls your name to make it stay.

A Letter Home

I long for a comfort that cannot be measured,
forgotten caves where Bach can't reach,
the bell that sounds for a monarchy
not found on any globe, for the feverish
gathering of hunters who oil
and polish their guns. I long for the salt
that tears contain, the marrow that boils
in my bones, long for the miracle opening up
like a mouth when nothing comes out.
If I am the only one listening, the percussion
of grace in my loins is what I become,
pulling the trigger like no one has taught me
and no one would know how to prevent.
Alone on a trail that no map contains
I follow the line of your neck. Your head
is tilted back, I give myself to whatever it is
that strains my muscles and forces me
to bloom like a rifle going off,
scattered and joined in a single place,
my Rome, Medina, Jerusalem.

The Carefree Boy

The clouds are sagging with rain,
lightning dissolves into the indigo sky.
A bell rings and keeps ringing
in a votive shrine at the crossroads.
On a path overgrown by bramble and bush,
grass blades sting my palms, but I
can withstand it, I who nurse
a passion with my mouth, your naked shoulder.
I lean over wooden fences, kneel for no reason
and nearly faint, the fervor inside my body
making music. Two martens flicker
to the forest edge. The moon has slicked
your back. Wherever I sleep, my body turns
to a spiral. It glides. Ancestors of shepherds
wake up within my dreams, unfold
their only cloak in front of me.
Meadows sheared by wind, fern, thyme,
and ringlets of dust. Later, by the pink lace
of a saturated sky. My blood thickened
at altitude, in labored, alpine air. I am a kid
with only one toy. I don't let go of it
as I wander through cities and plains,
handing myself over to what's ahead.

Revelation of Milk

It's uncomfortable to lean against
the round walls of the fountain.
But the peace a crying child demands
must dwell in every curve. This
is the first law. It has always been.
And so, the baby falls asleep
on his mother's breast, here and there
still sucking a little, sinking into slumber.
In the gap between two houses
on the square, the sea appears and fades
and reappears. The mother's tiny finger
glides along the edge of his mouth
to stop the drooling milk. The fortress
in Istria murmurs, a tree comes to life
out of stone, its roots hold to earth
tighter than desire. The tongue stirs.
I would like to try, the voice says,
soaked with a need to refuse the reign
of things, and frail as if not spoken
by the father. You move closer and kneel,
naturally, gazing into the blue of nipples
and breasts, their pale gleam stretched
like an olive before it gives oil.
A few hairs around them, like a faint light
at the end of a tunnel, the opening
of a channel you will go through.
The warm glow is inaccessible
until your final breath, and so airy
you easily surrender. Roads once
left behind in friends and books,
they disappear, and you recognize

that every drop is yours, as the woman
over you lifts the swollen fruit.

Nursing

She who removes from the countless
the solitude of their lives. She who,
in a single instant, calls upon the scattered salt
to return to bread's soft tissue, to harden memory.
She who boldly cups her breast
as if it were a glass she toasted with.
She who has made you the guest of honor,
you watch astonished as everything destined
to finish is granted its name and grows with her.
Rising like the first loaf of bread in the morning,
still damp around the ends, thawing in the mouth
the whole world opens up, from the lush hills
rising from a crumpled pillow to the entrance
at the base of the skull, to the garden and address
of this happy house. Without hurrying, the lips draw
their home around her nipple, which smells
of cream at the height of pleasure,
the world reaching out and holding you
like your mother used to hold you, long ago.

Mary Magdalene

The door closes behind me. A short hallway
I don't resist, as I did not decline your invitation
an hour ago. It came quite unexpectedly
amid the smoke, the worn-out armchairs,
the endless litanies of gain and loss. It came
with welcome urgency and added to my confusion,
which accompanies me, step by step,
as if it were hard to trust its outstretched arms,
the region of light, the swaying of a silver fir
in the arctic. As if thousands of years must pass before
here, in this very room, simple but far from slight,
it were possible to believe in you again.

Exercise for the Renewal of a Family Line

Small boats in the harbor, slack ropes
rest at evening, quietly whisking the poles,
but everything is as it should be, this calm.
Without it, impossible to feel the muscular
hand that stretches from above and from the side,
out of waves and out of air, heavy with pleasure
it reaches under me and carries me.
I am diffused along its endless fingers,
bloated sails inhale the wind, though
the time is not quite right. The mast begins
to crack when the stuff of prior miracles
stirs within, and the boat recoils across
the surface and drones like a shooting star,
hailing from a minor key, vanishing before
it's echoed off the face now emerging
from this foam. It agrees with me: in the warm sea
of membranes and marrow, the world is rising again.
Again, only one of us has an inkling of its shape.

Before a Throne

Wait for me, my lord, I would like
to stop, I would like to sit down,
to cross my legs and look
at nothing but you. Please excuse me,
but I would like to see you up close
from the top of a dizzying tower,
want to see myself as you see me,
you who take shelter in the flicker
of flat, impassive stars. You see a woman
dressed in a cotton shirt,
her talent for comfort, her loyal physique,
a woman who wants to make a home
in all this: let her, lord, in your huge hand
reaching toward the north, where it vanishes
like silver among the fish, in the no man's water
of the Atlantic. Maybe I myself will see her
just as I am seen, beneath a sky that fades
like a distant foghorn, alone in the world,
a garden of mandatory twilight.
While my family and children, playing
somewhere, slipped out of earshot
as you approached, you pressed against me
tighter than any need, entered and
devoured me in an instant that knows
no term. With a glue as white as dolphin fins
you splashed my forehead and face.
I would like, if only once, to see this as you do.

Blind

Don't leave me, don't run
cruel as lava across a continent.
Don't slip away like the shade of an arrow
into the writing, the wall. At nightfall
the presence of eyes, never to be forgotten
and big, like saying goodbye to a flag
and its many folds, delivered to your mercy
long ago—has it been years—
me, a fugitive, fleeing from mistakes,
rumors that turn into family legend
sure as the rain of embers turns
to stone. Don't leave me now
as my debtors have left me, don't send me
back to the foot of a cross, silent on a hill,
or to towns where I wandered
streets lined with trees, trying to forget
the boiling semen, looking for a refuge
in fur that itches and dampens on the spot.
Don't leave me now, as I do not abandon
the harvest grapes, I smear them on you
wherever you tell me to. Every move
of your body a test, trying me and the truth,
your panting says you'll stay here
after all. I give myself up, ask nothing.
I don't want to interrupt these hands
that steal, like gun smugglers, along the inner
arch of your thighs, these rare moments
between. I bend by the law only you
understand, tenderness to the tight cord,
multiplied by a hundred under the eyelids
you shine and take my sight away from me.

Property Lines

I breathe beneath the blanket, this space is mine,
and mine the sigh when we are alone together,
I mark it so there is no mistake, mark the excitement
of valleys and canyons rippling along our sheets.
I exercise the right to mark my space. I walk downstairs,
this space is mine, a scent, a trace, my palm in the air
above the banisters, I watch you in the garden, this space
is mine, how you stretch and, for the last time today,
dig the soil under some wilted peonies.
Simple chores deceive me, I want to adjust my senses
to the wavelength of a song slipping through a window
in too short a breath, this space is my own, or so I say,
in love with modest shapes, clean and quiet and smaller
than your desire which knows no limit, pressing on
as messengers who long to get to where they must.
This space is mine, I am at home in the gaps between words,
in trills of falling, falling hair I twist around my body,
in this house, it is mine, this dream, it is mine,
this face that talks back to the mirror,
like a rip in all things that should be there
so a beam of light will keep streaming in,
light in this space that is no longer mine
covering you and me, you and me.

Christmas in America

The heat is rising already, daybreak
reddening only for you, who smile as if
everything's clear ever since you left
your longing behind: arcades, palaces,
the town where you woke in a lavish December
and entered the house of a man,
sunlight caressing the bricks with love
and daring plans for a birth that doesn't end.
The heat is rising, a clang from the tower—
no, this is not the church where
five years old in ballet slippers
you saw, for the first time, a child
making his forceful way, like a piece of fruit
alone in the fields, drawing a comet to itself,
shining at dawn. The heat is rising, the choir sings
a hymn in a language we do not speak:
sound fills the space without stopping,
rises like a river, a pelvis, trained to get
the better of soldiers and mastering its exercises
with lesser prophets and Flemish painters.
One thrust of your hips and they're all
back from the dead, this moment is split
between us, rapture and no regret
in the heat of what we hunger for.

The Year 2000

The youngest of the sisters was the first
to extend her hand. The smell of grated lemon
and a bluish gas encouraged the flames,
the fire. It was around Christmas,
an old carpet, the family had lived here
for several generations. Whoever wishes,
as newcomers often will, can still inscribe
a line, quickly do the math of pro and con
before clearing out, never to return.
But it is late. And while the moment
does not expire, I can't make it linger:
this is the comfort given by a woman
up on her tiptoes, touching the highest branch,
the room has started to flicker at dusk,
and as in a poster shot, a lamp is lending its twilight
to the tree. An angel has claimed a forked twig
for his private kingdom. And his brothers
are invited to exit their boxes, come out
of their holsters, out of the stores that held them back
all year long, and spread their wings again
like an open book, like you, a woman with fewer
memories than a star has specks of dust.
It's good enough to cover you, it sings
without making a sound.

Last Resort

I like to go bareheaded, stick out my tongue,
I've got no interest in clay or how it's handled,
and obey the law, if I can understand it.
I accept it like singing, less often like dancing,
an annual holiday. Since you've shown me
the narrow path to safety, my hope has grown.
Give me the loyalty nature lacks, give me
a chill in the bones to call out like a child. I will strike
like a camera's flash through comma after comma,
through fog as it covers the fen. Can't you make
an exception? Give me a life unlike other lives
which have to spell out the sky, make me move
vertical instead, into the porous earth:
an engine forces me downward, no stopping,
it drills a hole in the capillaries, almost
imperceptible and bent on serving you,
on licking you as if you were resin
the pilgrims were greedy for, in the poppy fields.
I put my tongue inside you to prove—as if
you needed proof—that you are not alone
when it floods you where you want. There is
only one world. I guard it without remorse.

Persistent Storm

A coastal wind blows cold around the corners,
so passionate, so strange, it cannot arrive
any other way, the shirt and scarf are torn
from my body, it rushes my bones and enters
electric lines, turning orchards to ash.
But there is no choice: now and then
a storm from the south imports a draft
of despair, dying down and leveling off
to routine. Only the beauty of extremes
can dissent, that and maybe a little flame
in the center, in a circle where we dance.
There's no choice: I will be orphaned
if I spit out what surprises my own throat,
if I am too quick, don't get around to holding
back the miracle in my mouth, or between
the hips of a naked self, weightless
and letting the light pass through
like during a dance, a final round for me
and the rest of my tribe. I must get up,
must run for all those who sleep alone,
run and keep running in spirals, in sweat,
all the way down to the base of the spine
which bows like a mast in the storm,
driven into the gulch between two waves
that finish off whatever is left of the breath.

A Bath before Bed

If I pull back, because I can't stand
how pain can only recognize more pain,
it will come after me, dark and shivering
with a power I feel even now: this rhythm
one part peace and one desire,
tempo made in the image of prayer
will be looking for me,
will find me in a town without a name,
where beggars and sinners
who want to be kids again
are chased away, the watchman
shooing me from the fountain.
My throat is dry, I understand
even less than before.
Less and less certain that a piece
of the past is alive, even now,
in some cellar below the mind,
insisting like an oath to the secret
that makes me rinse your back,
up and down, a familiar stroke,
a damp cloth over your hips,
the soapy water rising to steam
and softening me like clay
that works and in its joyful task
is done. Today, at least,
a tiny grace is mine.

Columbus

I am a well-oiled rudder in your hands,
my will a beeswax candle wick. I hardly
ever burn without your consent.
I stand before you where many have stood,
a violence in my veins, I'm ready to drown
and chew on coral, the sandy ocean floor,
my future only a hint in front of me:
just say the word and a sounding line
will plumb the deepest part
where trembling is a form of salvation.
Like Moses faced with water that won't
give way, waiting to be divided before
it covers all there is with oblivion,
inviting me by its odor, its color,
the shape it sets itself. Gathering
what little remains of my strength
and overflowing the edge, I rip your
cloak with my teeth. As a caravel
missing its compass and crew
will find its own way back to port,
I follow an order to anchor in this alcove,
saliva coating the wharf
at the small of your back.

The Promised Land

A secret, like thunder off in the distance
and a flower made of lead. It hisses
and hardens in water, this secret I want to savor
for a long time. Even longer. Longer, even,
than I can see while staring across the plains,
across the herd asleep between your legs
and the broad wall of your back,
stopping along the rim of a constellation.
To stick my tongue out awkwardly,
making the flavor mine, yes, this is
what I want: with every move
to be gathered into myself, ripe for the planet
rescued from forgetting and rendered new
as it veers into orbit and hovers there.
It will flood your pores with the salty
smell of shells, and adopt the night.

Cast Vote

That crystal morning, snow over snow:
in capital cities they might be ashamed of it.
That conference of birds, and light upon water,
the parliament of dreams that knows no fear
of getting old, and she, alone this winter
morning, her face that sees itself within
a flower etched by ice along the glass,
her reflection thawing and piercing
the window: is she really so strange?
Outside, her shadow sputters again
like a match refusing gravity and singe.
In the vast expanse of frost and worry,
not even a minute to think, she was the one
with the courage to disobey silence, disobey
orders, she could not be voted down and said:
Look, in the shallows of this common river
the Black Sea claims as its own,
fish still wriggle out of a boy's hands, tracing
a nearly perfect arc, and with them everything
that flows, everything that falls, rushes
without reason as one's childhood rushes by—
look: we are not a wall but a shutter
some far-off god is opening halfway.

UNDER THE WATERLINE

for you, this time without hesitation

I. Habits of Heavy Rain

Sobering Up

Old men sleep near dogs in hallways, ignored
like past dictatorships, the dream of everything

that might have happened. Hey, lord,
what of my longing to look,

in dark palace bedrooms, at masters
decaying in saddles on the top decks of the Nina,

Maria and Pinta. I feel the soft salt
of the Atlantic under my feet, and people

stare at me, an intruder of sorts, surprised
and propped on the steps of their houses,

I'm no less startled to see in the backdrop
a void that gapes beneath the Southern Cross.

Residents wearing crimson shawls
count rosary beads and forecast the future

from bones of tribes long gone. Elevators
inside the glass towers in courtyards

sidle down and up, never reaching a tip
for ideas of fame and bravery to take off.

Passengers on this circular ride, idle for hours
at a time, stare as the walls go sliding by,

not touching them. They hide from each other
what binds them. O to arrive, on horseback or camel,

over mountains and the pale green Sargasso,
to this town where oddballs and stammering

philosophers are protected by the law
against disdain. They're drained by now

like a plant under hot sun, a rotting flower,
a fine daze, they could do with fresh water,

their lips are chapped and dry, and swell,
stiffen in shock like an empty

pitcher's echo. Today your name
is listened to for the last time.

Hometown

Thousands of fountains, slender jets of water
invite the sea into reveries of walkers, a sea

not too far away, to gush through a hidden mouth,
envelop every street, every tree in the sparse

grove of Tivoli, every arcade and corridor with
a brittle crust, a bounty of salt, a trace dissolves

and disappears inside the granite cobbles. The sea
is here, the sea is here, a furious streaming through

peepholes in doors, stoic triumphal arches: it doesn't
care for the coolness of hills only an arm's reach off,

let alone for untanned girls, whose bodies, for a moment
or two, flash through the reeds, down below Mount Krim

where the marshland sponges up time, and the fern veins
sweat with the stars. Rushes in still waters hum against

the canals, piercing the faint light under the door,
for the last time here for a woman heaving with effort,

her nimble amber body pushing the lamp's flame away,
restless to bear the air that flickers with steam: it's

an order to stone the newcomers. Who could separate
fear from skin and bones? No one, not even the natives.

They've gotten what they deserve: a collective
nightmare that's dragged itself into the house

and forced the flowers open, until they spit out
bugs. I'm not surprised that the marble head

of the cavalier is drowning in bog. I'm waiting
for the stars' sweat to dry, for the ships moored

beneath the town castle since the age of Jason
to raise their sails again; and the governor's palace

falls victim to the illusion it can still reign in
the harmonies and the clattering masts, when thieves

and liars, every last one our kin, set sail for
the island out of legend. They take a secret with them.

We're left with only disgrace. The fortress walls
stay quiet about it; I can't: in the name of the people,

I have a feeling that a voice faster than a falcon
will punish us, will split our skulls in two.

Hungary, Near and Alone

Tramway tracks, laid before the last war,
lead to high houses on the main square:

nowhere else. At open windows sheets
shine white, blood specks the edges,

women wave goodbye at evening,
a farewell from jealousy moves me,

a lonely fantasist. I take an interest in shells
of the succulent mouth, my neighbor's mostly,

she pushes her breasts into nightfall, from
the shelter of her balcony she listens

to a storm disturb the surface of the lake,
bending over engravings I can't afford,

that's why I trust in accidents of charity,
the necessity of a song in a language with

no relatives. Veterans, cheated by memory,
stare in confusion across reeds of Lake Balaton,

how it rises and turns, trying to become
a sea again, it weeps in defeat under

lilac bushes shushing into bloom
with a violet shirr, and a mad piano player

fondles the keys, the alcohol helps,
knitting notes for masters from before.

To Help a Friend

The tint on the stony skin of the Venus
of Willendorf dissolves in wells of rainwater

swollen under the gutters of Alpine ridges.
Small comfort for the water heads in a city

by a river. You ride no horse.
Imagine if you will the Pannonian plains

and the quiet sobbing of boys with their lips
lapis black from kisses forced on them.

It makes no sense to speak to them of perfection.
Can you hear horses? No? I didn't think so.

You prefer silence under a whip,
the shush that follows old aunts

when they shimmy across the Grabenstrasse,
past shop windows with their maps sown

in human skin and books about slender officers;
honor has run them into death, a death better

than the fear of holiday tedium no ceremony
can keep away. The whip swishes stale air

and points a painful way to the homes
of people made of mud, folks who keep on

living through common guilt. I can't
do anything but toss the last poppy harvest

into the river, which threatens to flood its
cemented banks. In an instant I forget chestnuts

in cinders, kneel in wet sand on a shore
and shape a ship: it will prove itself

on its maiden journey, and the last one
when your time is up. Clear water sluices

my fingers, along the skin of breasts,
don't move now, down the eternal belly

to the aureoles, my tongue tastes them
like berries in winter, under the vault

of a Capuchin crypt, where a violent tsar has
called the desperate together for one battle more.

Ten Years After

I travel alone, I envy the pack, which
like the Slavic people whose exit to the sea

only Shakespeare dared to recognize
is now drowning in a delta that has

flooded the trail to the watchtowers,
the boundless sky of pale blue, which I see

but don't share family with. How it tenderly
drops and fades away into light, warm and

generous. It can't help itself: it has to honor
the profiles of curves and flaxen hair on

the façade of town hall, coax shadows
of hop groves to the bar, set up in a courtyard.

Avenues of lindens and of young women
spread with a quiver, always at someone

else's service, a sigh throttled in throats
of tamed shrews. A memorial plaque

on the mansion broken to pieces of a Latin
sentence doesn't want to disown the scars

incurred by bowing exercises, clasped
hands and a finger crossed in a pocket.

I warn you I travel alone, envy the pack,
and if you want to follow me you have to

go on foot, your eyes fixed only ahead,
because you decide nothing, although you

may take notes: from Saturday to Thursday
you do it well, the black glass of tears drips

into your chronicles of the land whose fleet
is moored in spires under the mildew

of the Baroque. Then you start to gargle,
so quick and forceful that a stutter is half

the battle, and finally no noise. Lucky you,
now you have a secret known by a poet

with lung cancer and a legend, a secret
I've designed for you if you want to

travel with me, wordless, your face
facing into a breeze, about to ask

if October might last another day.

Prague, fall 1999

Dresden Under Water

Under ripped shirts and tableaus by old painters,
cold as the muffled speech of an early winter,

we murmur a torrent's melody together, it breaks
through cracks in the cobbles of Frauenkirche,

swelled with memories of those who've drowned
or left for other towns, where little girls jump rope

alone and children, dressed in Sunday best, sob in
untended gardens. We look through a slit in the wall,

into screens, past dams and the fingers of a human chain
with buckets as heavy as wet coats, cowslips shot into

blossom, where bike trails were, past the acrid odor
of sinking earth. I'd rather turn away, to not be seized

by guilt, but there's no way: my eyes are asters of summer
escaping, they rot in fields in tall bundles. I can't take it,

pour me another. Good, thank you. I feel better now.
Invisible to my relatives, who dream up stars in a blue sky,

I open my arms and invite myself to a woman who rises,
naked or nearly, from sands on the eastern shore.

II. Liquid Dreams

Escape from an Insane Asylum

I'm a former sleepwalker, partly cured,
but this doesn't stop me swimming like a fish

that swallowed the ocean inside my dream.
A quick check, the knife is there, it's related

to shadows of newly skinned prey, and I learn
to tell the future from pools of blood: to gather

chrysanthemum hats means sickness no medicine
fixes; to hold a flute of hazelwood in your hands

beckons virtue; to talk with frozen water, the coming
of wealth from afar; to undress a woman down

to the string between her buttocks while she sleeps,
a temporary seizure; to bring wine to boil and bathe

in a brook, this is being honest. To eat the bark
of a tree, or praise, or swear like an auto mechanic, it means

to be free. A school of fish has grown wings, they guide
me through storms and illusion books, I keep watch

to miss nothing that matters, I get thin as the horizon's
blade, somewhere else, my god, the nonsense isn't lost

on me, nor the ice-skate down the corridor
with grids on all the windows, despite myself

I turn into sticks of wax that slick my track past
drowsy guards, they couldn't care less, I miss

them by only a hair, a sliver of bliss on my cheek;
outside the ocean goes frantic, and somber glass

in the wall breaks, and I find myself
in a country where the girls perfume their palms,

to read the signs of long ago and know they
speak of home. Me, I can't decipher them.

Tattoo under a Bridge

They've burned images into your skin,
they leave black traces—volcano ash—

that fade to fertile soil, covering wounds
and dusting the curious mouth, images

from a private collection—here a burial
ground of beached whales, there the first

verse of a hunting song, or the Gobi Desert
bisected by a line between

the borrowed and occupied banks,
like a river under the bridge of your breasts,

in vain it foams beneath the throat,
finds no alliance with moments of mercy,

success on opening night, pleased
with itself like a sky without stars

or rival, as long as you live it will trickle
from the spring in your right ear's shell

and empty into the left, eddying over
the fields of muscle and over the knolls

of the weathered face I'm fascinated by,
will lift like a statue sculpted of honey—dark,

sweet, and gummy—and seal my eyes; your body
quavers, and nothing is hid. Take me, I'd like

to lie down in the riverbed and bathe myself
in water that runs to the rhythm your breathing makes.

Sticky Silk

Your head tilted back. A fat plum opens.
Lightning strikes in the nerves

and veins, all the way to the tongue, the brain,
it's beautiful and rare like a Lebanese cedar,

the horizon froths and frays; and arms spread wide
with surprise and a gift, whose meaning remains

unknown to us both, like music that slithers
the straits between the cushion and the curtain.

Draw it apart, push out the shutters: tin soldiers
were left in the garden when the young recruits

barreled in, maybe to call it a night, between
covers of favorite picture books, into the warm

rooms of evening where the floors are covered
in fleece of fed sheep, digesting grass with no

shepherds around or fear of sparrow hawks.
They circle low to force the price in flesh,

full of amazement. You summon it, veiling
the sky with threads of sticky silk.

Terra Mobilis

Look, a stone promontory: it kisses
a distant shore, the crack between day

and night is expanding, and insects
without names are buzzing, sleepless.

They are bothered by the heat of two
bodies, naked in the liquid southern breeze.

Our pupils harden and the tongue comes
to know the taste of resin. We're needy

as the Bible needs a reader, as smooth
as a fishbone and breasts

before birth, and as for the fallen
leaves—these I'd like to stencil

at the confluence of thighs and write
an excuse for the mild madness of me,

seconds before the sweet end,
when the unspent shivers on old

peoples' faces call again to youth.
The eleventh commandment forbids it,

I know, but how to hold back?
Be quiet, swollen member of the team,

no one can tell you apart from
the veiny shrub resembling a pine:

they mimic each other, the flowing
that follows the flaws of a face.

Kamenjak, Istria, July 2000

Lesson of Darkness

A finger of light from above jabs me,
cold as an animal bone, it lights

up nothing, least of all a criminal,
a victim, a witness: I have little trust

in the biographies of sun spots, more
in dusk. In the sheltering dark I can ask

when a tree becomes a stone, when stone
is eroded to statue. For some this stays

an enigma, like the dream of an artist who
makes birds out of bank notes, while for me,

who meanders like a river that hasn't found its
channel, I imitate smiles on children's faces.

For me it's important that the people and things
I see inside a shining mirror saturate the space,

and its glass, dried in the wind, guarantees
that a feature film and documentary show

my life on a single reel, this strange image
that might illuminate solitary people

in the cinemas where they hide before
a vertigo slaps them, a finger of light

in the heart of the home, broadened
by the stairways and mistakes. They

live humbly, like lichen up north, and
there's nothing they'd commit to, nothing

they'd do for each other, strung like wires
that attach the trams to sky in Budapest.

Underneath, a cruel angel stands with legs
apart, cold as animal bone, in a shirt,

cut to measure, he won't take no for
an answer, telling me to quit writing

and admit, sorry to say: the only story
that really counts, that one I can't finish.

A Sunday Dilemma

A town square, a cave of damp salt,
the snow has stopped falling, bladed cold,

the street is quiet, pedestrians in and
out of arcades, like skimming on waves

in the republic of water, ice crystals
under the night lamps focus their

lack of shape, disheveled rooms wheeze
in extinguishing light. Loner uncles read

magazines, their covers covered in black
foil, and love, this little-known thing,

feeds on the calories of detail, it sucks
them out of the final marrow, an animal

marking its territory, I hear a noise that's
not yet words, a leg along another leg,

maybe too quick for my taste, but I want
to be there, feel the feathered arches of your

ribs, every breath will trigger a flood of blood
above the lobes I want to lick, I have to say,

somewhere on the Turkish side of Cyprus,
in towns that keep their shame to themselves,

again I return to the surface to breathe,
above the frame of the screen: out the window

with it, then, it hasn't yet revealed if I'm
a storm tomorrow, or today a lightning bolt.

III. Tattered Net

Urgent Questions

Frogs stand guard. They sit without
moving, don't waste their strength

when down the river patches of vegetation
flow to plait a carpet, soft and suffocating

like towns that grow, step by step,
and threaten to flout all thresholds.

This matters: it concerns me
and everyone who comes to stand

on my behalf, singing praise
to a king. I extol him because

he made the monasteries bid goodbye
to pride. Scribes, stoned on hallucinations

of Gibraltar and the Hebrides carry out
their duty: to forget defeat and draw

swords again, to conquer useless land
and the plains and islands baptized

by ancient blades and licked by fire
and smoke, to wet with the amber

saliva of travelers sand stuck between
the teeth, like a question that has to be

asked just as menstrual blood is necessary.
Do we inherit only a character, or the story

itself as well? When did the memory
of the clan fall asleep? Have we managed

to turn misfortune to virtue? Have fish
fossils swum up through the underground

rivers to the Alps? Do people, blind since
birth, dream the explosion before dawn

and the warning voice that echoes across
the monarchy? Does a birch grove equal

the kind of sadness old as pilgrimages
to Compostella? Is there anyone left

who remembers how a handful
of dreamers by vocation used to saunter

through labyrinthine streets without
a clue, singing ballads and strewing

images of a girl who lifts her skirt
and wakes the soft god back to life,

who had earlier refused to obey?
They hung out in front of the cinema

doors, were spotted inside the Europa Café,
their breaking voices reminders

of the gilded books where
all things splendid, all things noble

happen in a fever that frets—how
the crime assumes a beautiful silhouette.

White Nights in the South

Lights, countless lights: a beam of floodlight
siphons past you standing by a window

then drops to flame on the far side of dark
and signals flare in blushing cheeks and fairy

tales on Christmas Eve, on and off again the lights,
hovering webs of lit-up windows, balls of sparks

and towers and palaces, built with no time
to waste. You follow it, how it traces the ground.

The eye can only guess at what a hard kiss
does: it pulls the lord away from things

and lets the blood from a soul. But you, it
deepens you, with no fake solace caresses you,

the North Pole light that's finally found its
way—I know this, ribbons of light and of flags

flying, they flutter over the flower markets,
city alleys and citizens eating from each

other's hands. That's why we want
to flicker here too, this barely light

that lifts the buttercups, big as silver
coins: you buy one, take home two.

False Hope

On the night of October sixteen, a hurricane raged
across the isles on the other side of the channel,

it had been raining all day, weathermen
overlooked a maelstrom that came up out

of whirlpools churning Biscay Bay, disgraced
the harbor and sent hormones of imagination running

a hundred miles an hour; they blustered along
the ropes between houses, on pulleys and through

a woman's image taking her laundry up to a terrace,
a hand hilted there on her hip, pointing the way

of the wind northeastward, toward cliffs without
moss, early in the morning on a coast that moans

when the first blow comes and lorries are flitted,
roofs spread out their wings, and bats flutter from

belfries into a grid of dark tracks on a dark sky,
the sky spells a message in dark; but who,

who would read it now, when bedrooms are swept
by the stench of a sick man, forgotten by everyone,

a faint smell of carmine from cave paintings on
the continent, winds that braid a colossal tangle

above the amorphous mass—fear prevents it
untying into a map, charted long ago—stink

of damp cigarettes and of blood, hot as the air
that pulses through my swollen pupils, which widen.

Cattle lick themselves around their muzzles, hurry
home, dogs graze the grass, it's a month of rain,

fog, cold, when only shiny mushrooms at night
attract a few animals, the veins in my arms

are knotted, grab into empty space—there's
nothing to do but watch, count down, it's

the month of hail, downpour, sleet, there's
nothing else to do but watch, and hope that

every season seeks its end. That the month of heat,
and harvest, and fruit will enter the years again.

Stone and Flame

All the days had ripened
before that last. It was lightning,

not a beetle, that burned a zigzag
into the bark. A constellation goes

out the moment it's flared. The second
Rome is on fire. He weighs this detail

like a peach, until it rots. She says:
the sickness is bad, only a few have

been spared. It seems she knows
humiliation and warmth in the places

I also know, but it's best I stay
unconscious. Let her speak.

I've got nobody, she says, to give
him what I had and lost: a smooth

stone my tribe has passed from mouth
to mouth in repeated stages of silence,

when the mute tongue caresses
and cleans and tumbles the pebble,

white, from the Sava's banks,
to be licked its length and across,

as the ancestors taught us to.
If you're sad, wet it courageously,

if overcome by happiness
take it between your teeth.

A memory can kick up
more than a man expects, the flock

is startled and feathers, a million
of them, whirl in a choir that wants

to cover lines of magma and bristling
skin that suffers the nails, how

they stitch it in a last convulsive grip,
on the last day, when we do as our

lineage told us to, writing on the wall,
in rupture, the name of the arsonist.

Dream, Write, Erase

This poem is a form of disorder. Not even
an angel can manage it, much less me,

aimless pilgrim on a morning
in May, alone and still a little fresh

from the milk I've drunk, a sleepwalker
on dawn's edge. Ha, I squeezed it out of

a juicy poppy, halfway from Galicia to Bukovina,
as close to the sky as it gets and to the grilles

of speech, convinced no one can see me
at first light, which has merged the plains

of fog to dried up seas. I'm drinking a beverage
better than Red Bull, the flower smells sweet

on a wild stem, or a wild soul, while those grown
in gardens, for comfort, have fruit whose fragrance

seduces and oozes through the terrain, the very
place I'd like to go, on the run from armies

before the sergeant orders the village razed,
and a child's scream cuts the air cleansed of

the pointless litany would well up from my lungs
if I knew how, but I'm useless, like a net

in tatters, left to follow the edicts of the discipline
stick, a chocolate drop, keep my dreams to myself.

Time for a Change

On the river's surface, islands of ice,
they open passages, stitch them up,

winds canvass the piers and migrate
south. There's no excuse: I waste hours

of my mother tongue unable to remember
the body, soft as the fur of unborn martens,

lithe along the lower back and long,
long legs. When the traffic light changes

the skin is aflame and the naked shoulder arcs,
and the flutist's finger stretches in a gesture

that, to ordinary people, would signify
a greeting: the light from a street lamp

limps to the trees and I wonder where
the girl has gone who flirted with dusk,

darkling and bluish, awhile now no longer
green. Grass, green of the grass, the green

of a silk blouse, of closed eyelids and
marbles on a playground between the houses

in the sun, where pigeons flutter, not knowing
Mount Ararat from the nearby hill, its

graveyard of stony mouths, each one will listen
close tonight, to clue in weak signals, for an hour

or so, use what appears in the ice's malaise,
maybe break a flatbread with some strangers.

IV. Home Turf

Indebted to Ancestors

> The fruit is blind. It's the tree that sees.
> —René Char, *Leaves of Hypnos*

Drizzle under the slender arch,
I lean against the facades to keep dry

but droplets tumble vertical and there
is no solution: I find refuge in the first

portico, locked, lean against the door
and wait it out. I can't go anywhere,

am stuck with this assignment:
honor the killed who are waiting

for us, unburied under every hill
and under the granite walks; I'm

left to ask to turn into salt, which
lasts indifferent, calm. I'd default

on the debt to the ancestors for good:
instead of the shudder of the regiment,

I'd prefer to speak, in vain, how a man
might become a child again, and have

a hunch about windows in walls, whistle
in the catacombs at a flock of fumbling

swallows, homing in on their nests,
longing for Saturdays when the murmur from

the gorge is celebrated, where nobody suffers
from hunger or thirst any more. On an empty

stomach I'm shaky in love among relatives,
as painful as a revelation: I've nowhere to go,

an unwilling witness. Hold a minute, don't think
worse of me: I make my own bed, my sister

kneads dough, I send my sons to the barber.
Isn't it enough? Well, then: in secret I listen

to idols, will even admit this if pressed,
will ransom the captives inside the abyss,

because a man hears often what he'd rather not,
if once he wants to have his way and says it.

Exile

Like lover's juice spat by a woman
for hire, they're driven by desperate,

radiant light, far away and down on
deserted plains, toward columns

of people traveling, tired, past the ruins
of town hall and the cathedral, past stone

walls that barely differ from rocks
themselves, covered by moss, past

the meadows where walking is forbidden.
Crossing the former trenches, the weakest

among them had seen the towers of smoke
rising from camp fires below the forest line.

Their translucent eyes reflect only shadows
of clouds gliding over the narrow trails

they walk down, conjuring pastures and
fertile valleys, moments of sheer delight,

they dream of large estates, expertly manicured.
Water sources camouflaged by the coarse

surfaces of rocks, they stand at the edge
of the steep ravine that flats their echo out,

like an indifferent god with slack fists,
and dazed. They keep their eyes closed,

on a fragile crag they take off their jackets,
patched together of rough flax, and lie down

on their backs, in comfort, their vests
slither over their heads, their trousers

over their ankles drop to a quivering pile.
They lie naked under familiar gray.

In the narrow funnel of mountains they see it,
for the last time: drugged women and children

with faces of stillborn animals, the big moon above,
small village below, and me—we all need to know why.

A Design for Mutiny

The level of the Drava is dropping,
the moon waxes, the towers of the only

bridge exhibit their fissures when we,
the lost, gather together, at one in our

inability to return the gaze of the capital's
ruler, as the infinite armies who serve him

can and do. Not us: we keep to the code
of an evening sigh that doubles as a farewell,

keep to instructions obliging us, in the house
of the women we've come to pick up,

to shake hands with their fathers and keep our
commentary to ourselves, dressed to the nines,

though mountain women who read our thoughts
would tell us to wear only black, like a forest dark,

and dark the lament that wears away the early
morning air in the square, as the edges on

the facade of the Astoria Hotel reveal a tainted
origin, at the bottom of collective memory;

it sings in the inner ear of the night porter
as the fossils shimmer under plaster, then a siren

shatters the sonic wall and we step back, the lost
ones, knowing the sound from our knotted hands,

in a single blade of grass: a whole generation
whistles against it, until the bridge has collapsed.

The Secret Brotherhood

Welcome, sailors, figs, the scent of psalms,
welcome, all who understand that we discover

the sound of our native songs elsewhere, like a thing
that belongs to us without having to earn it. Welcome.

Nothing happens in an instant, neither the stylish
mask for a landscape, well rehearsed in catastrophe,

nor the boys who have outgrown wet nurses,
though still enthralled to softness, to be protected

against the fact that a man is less than nothing
without the river bend that responds when called

by name, a man at home everywhere, in mirrors
and in the ebb and flow of changing tides

that dissolve the pain of the disinherited, like
the pallor of yellow flames, the many forms of goodbye,

in the zenith when the sea unfolds under a seagull's
nest on Olive Street, where I copy treatises on river

pools, on supple women's hips before being touched,
to calm the apparitions, ruined capitals and people,

mad like me, who dream the eyes of bloodhounds,
their saliva drops to the ground and their hair bristles

the sky. The accordion player is playing a wild song
of the secret brotherhood from Porto Allegre, as close

as my jugular this wake-up anthem and drinking jingle,
taken for his own by a man returning from the French

foreign legion; he's not asleep, he watches the processions
of roughly hewn coffins, stares blank back to the distorted

faces and the deserts reaching after him from the long gone
days of pleasure, back to the young daydreamer who hasn't

yet tasted figs and doesn't know the local tune, in order
to lure him with a clandestine map of the beach where

he first drew his slingshot and made a mark. We are guilty.
We kept quiet about the echo, returning now as cannon fire.

A Report on Defeat

The soldiers, soaked to the waist,
stand in ditches, leaden roe swirls

like sentry passwords in cold air
and resin runs out of the nostrils

of horses from the rearguard battalion.
With the first snow we withdraw

to the growing towns, every day
more refugees swarm in

and the memorial to the unknown prostitute
is unveiled, like Napoleon's obelisk.

A crowd gathers underneath, hungry
and lewd, and nobody sees how the little

door in the wooden clock opens, and instead
of a cuckoo now a living bird dashes out

and leads the way into the suburbs,
which multiply as fast as fake paintings where

only a baby's eye could spot that it is not blood,
red as Karst wine, but love the newcomers bring,

the love for films with no narrative and no
short sequences, heroes sporting long hair

and beards that wait for winter to go,
wait for the day when again they'll trade

in passion and dreams, relentless waiting,
a full-time job, on the vigilance of the people

who want beauty to be necessary, necessity
beautiful, among them I who have shed

the uniform of the defeated army so I can
devote myself to the exercise of a skill that

grants no diplomas: with no food or drink
and a smuggler's stash of grass,

I burn eternal fire under the monument,
alone in a polar dark, though elbowed

by the crowd, I believe until the end
and, blind and happy, don't regret a thing.

The Night Shift

Water in the radiator gurgles, the radio
clacks like a sugar spoon. A coin, flipped

in air, doesn't come down. Virgins, we can
live with what we don't know. There are

few things, in fact, we know as well as
the first day of summer. We welcome its

disfigured form, the countdown starts in June.
Huh, what else are we left with? To launch

airplanes folded from yesterday's papers,
let them cruise across the clouds and breach

the Roman wall, then to unfold them
and flatten the pages, a hand will calm

the turbulence, to lie on a carpet and layer
the newsprint over the face, a secret rite

familiar to dream collectors in Madagascar
and Kranj, for a moment under a dome there comes

the voice of a woman who talks
about bubbles, until a blade of grass has

pierced them through, and crystals leak
from the screen before we're forced outside

as well: not one of us will remember how
a doe once drained a creek dry

up in the mountains somewhere, or words distilled
to images, puddles of resin I can't read,

waiting for the copper coin to drop
and decide: the night watch, that's me.

V. Solitary Fruit

Poor Substitute

Branches of a bush diffusing its scent of mountain
meadows, a hand goes through the hedge: it's here.

Our long lost brother watches windows
and, directing us to look up, we follow his

gaze to high above, into the indigo sky.
Together we all acknowledge the sudden

desire: to shatter the glass again and flutter up,
the stress in the groin sustains its pressure,

fearful of lust we gather as a flock, our eyes
closed, stand on tiptoe with little better to do,

seal our lips to the glass. We are distant kin,
orphans and prodigal sons, who open the bedroom

doors and glide down corridors, submerged
in moonlight striking the lips and cheeks,

onto last month's magazines, the carpet,
across the back of the armchair, a girl forged

of doorknocker brass who carries a bucket
with no bottom, constant as a migraine, restless

as desire, embers sift over the roofs of our
neighborhood, replace our heartbeat with names

of the lost, who have found a home somewhere else,
as a brother finds his sister—it's her I think of,

maybe you do too, when muscle tightens in a silver
line. I'm sorry no one noticed her out here.

No Choice

And half tenderly, half lazily,
With a kiss you brushed my hand—
And the eyes of mysterious, ancient faces
Gazed at me...
        —Anna Akhmatova, "Confusion"

A sound comes up from the northern woods,
dark and sugary. Maybe, I think, not sure,

it's only a goshawk. Yet maybe, just maybe
a Russian boy who jumped off the top of a tree

with his umbrella open, like sky above steppe,
and landed to the applause of the grass and,

without skipping a beat, picked up a tremulous
tune. I have to pass it on—but how? I'm not

saying it doesn't make sense to stay at home
between books and the kids, yet I tend to forget

it escapes me, the summer league results,
for example, but I remember a teapot of clay

and the perfect patchwork stains on its circular
lip. I cover them with my tongue. I'm as precise

in my daily routine as the bell of a suburban
church, of equal ease to travelers and locals,

hatching plans for action among the extended
evening shadows. Yes? No? I don't know, I have

no idea. All I know is that butterflies, freed
from tapestries, would not survive on their own, unless

guided by a sound, dark and saccharine, spreading
fast as the common flu, turning into a signpost

for paper peddlers pedaling through alleys of trees,
these postmen of lightest sleep, as the dead poet

would have said, tossing out rolled-up bundles
of news, subscribers can't read them, written

in the language of forgotten tribes who lived here
well before. They put their warriors in burial grounds

and committed their women to ash. They rule after death
and newspaper editorials keep praising them, until the cry

of a newborn breaks into guffaw. Yes? No? No choice.
Under an umbrella, I write the lines a soldier sings.

My Fear, Your Courage

We stay on the trail, but behind
the events. We have nothing but echoes

of our own voices, when we sat in front
of the fireplace, where three men sank

to easy sleep in cinders. Sunbeams flitted
on the wine glasses, we stared at the surface

of things inside their form, hardly disfigured
by agreeing on their names. It's enormous,

this world, huge with narcissistic thoughts
that evade a wayfarer's way, poised to take

in each and every courtyard as his own,
but a master only once a century or so.

While the others are in front of the fire,
in a coma since yesterday, I've gotten up,

all covered in sweat, again dreaming nuns,
who usher an end to travel at the door before

the zone of no return, on one side of the river
bank, same side every time. I'd prefer to show you

where, between the chimney and the eaves,
the warbler's nest, I'd fess up to small swindles,

entrust you with where a milk snake goes to get her
daily dose, on the threshold I don't dare to cross,

I'm straining my ears like a ram's horn, to catch
the chords the accordion bellows, elastic

and stretched by a crazy fellow, his sidekick sings along:
fear once put behind you is the start of being proud.

Ode to Wheat

They've axed the forests, plowed the meadows,
sown and sewed it up, task forces of tiny fingers

and hired hands are pruning back the cornflowers
that clamber and clamor for tenderness of sun

and water, for sympathetic looks without the help
of generations that celebrate the mother figure,

her lavish hips and license to give birth so
she need not fight any more, as she stands

in triumph among us, those who keep meat
on the menu, the love distilled in a spike

of wheat as the final measure of creation,
maybe even grace locked in a swollen grain.

Why would I lie to you? A harvest rots
right there on the ground, nobody feels like

carting it away. We prefer to fondle
the shiny blades and tears on the tips that

recall the etchings of provincial manors,
lost in the roiling mercury sea that stretches

across half the continent; stalks trickle out
of the baskets, leading from famished memory

to fertile soil. I doubt anything can move us,
least of all the order to pick it up and kiss it

should we let it drop. The competition between gain
and taste is ceaseless, and beauty falls by the wayside,

like a deserter who ducks the radar to prosper again,
multiplied a hundredfold, at the head of a huge

army that has laid its weapons down, and knees
bent enters the service of a goddess, pregnant

all the time, whose livelihood is gift and suffering.

Finger of Light

Memory: a blot in the archives of history,
luxuriant river backwaters and tributaries

for fishing by flashlight, at the Špica
where polliwogs grow into frogs

and gangs of wrestling boys are restless,
recollections, wordless signals, the fluid

of the finest narrative, which no one can
retell in full, that's why we pass it hand

to hand, respectful and inquisitive,
like a lid we lift slowly so not to be scalded,

the past doesn't care, the truth doesn't either,
whatever we think of them; the closer we get

the hotter it gets, that's clear; if I step back,
if you stay behind, the story is strewn,

the instant restarts, the finger of light winnows out
among willows, and now I'm left with what I've

never liked: a half hunch I was very close,
but what's it matter when I don't have a witness,

let alone answers to questions I switch on and off
like a feeble light, so many lamps in an empty house,

nervous that night won't fall any faster, I was quite
close to the collectors' camp, they know by heart

the chapters of this story drowned in croaking,
disappearing as circles do, on the surface of a lake.

The Frozen Monarchy

after Tomaž Šalamun,
A Ballad for Metka Krašovec

Deep below the bowels of a boat, cutting
through breakers no trouble, carting survivors

to god knows where, aware on a sunny day
of its sinking, so many years ago some have already

forgotten, you can see them: the cities
and piers, fun parks and parliaments, how they're

in line to be punished. They last in a spasm, locked
in shocking ice. It glimmers a shade of blue, the same

hue for everyone, for the looters of nests and altars
as for dandies with a finger on the trigger, deep down,

where slackened wishes to be forgiven have tacked
like metal to ice, with a grimace of pain. The oldest

would know the song, it sounds like a face
from the fairy tales, pronounces the prophets different

from despots, although they all feel the cold, save
those who wanted to save themselves by climbing

the slippery crests of a slope to shear the surface
and swim. There, an old captain my country admires

dances on deck in his bare feet, and buttons from
blouses and whitish teeth are sprinkled all around,

and I too forget what survives, how deep the wounds are
dug, and begin to speak like a river—a mouthful of mud.

Trieste—Vienna, September 2001

[the author]

Aleš Debeljak is a poet, literary essayist, cultural critic, and translator. The author of thirteen books of essays and eight books of poems in his native Slovenian, he has won the Prešeren Foundation Prize (the Slovenian National Book Award), the Miriam Lindberg Israel Poetry for Peace Prize (Tel Aviv), the Chiqu Poetry Prize (Tokyo), the Hayden Carruth Poetry Prize, and other awards. An Ambassador of Science of the Republic of Slovenia, Debeljak was also a Senior Fulbright Fellow at the University of California, Berkeley, a fellow of the Institute of Advanced Study at the Collegium Budapest, and Roberta Buffett Professor of International Studies at Northwestern University. He translated John Ashbery's selected poems into Slovenian, edited an anthology of American meta-fiction, and published a book of critical essays on American literature, while his own books have appeared in over a dozen languages. His poetry volumes in English are *The City and the Child* (White Pine, 1999, tr. Christopher Merrill), *Dictionary of Silence* (Lumen, 1999, tr. Sonja Kravanja), and *Anxious Moments* (White Pine, 1994, tr. Christopher Merrill). His scholarly works published in the United States include *The Hidden Handshake: National Identity and Europe in the Post-Communist World* (Rowman & Littlefield, 2004), *Reluctant Modernity: The Institution of Art and Its Historical Forms* (Rowman & Littlefield, 1998), and *Twilight of the Idols: Recollections of a Lost Yugoslavia* (White Pine, 1994). He lives with his wife and three children in Slovenia, where he directs the Center for Cultural and Religious Studies at the University of Ljubljana. He is also a recurring visiting professor at the College d'Europe, Natolin-Warsaw.

[the translators]

Brian Henry is the author of five books of poetry, most recently *The Stripping Point* (Counterpath, 2007). His translation of the Slovenian poet Tomaž Šalamun's *Woods and Chalices* (Harcourt) appeared in 2008.

Christopher Merrill has published four collections of poetry; translations of two books by Aleš Debeljak; several edited volumes; and four books of nonfiction, including *Only the Nails Remain: Scenes from the Balkan Wars* (Rowman & Littlefield, 2001). He directs the International Writing Program at The University of Iowa.

Andrew Zawacki has published three poetry books: *Petals of Zero Petals of One* (Talisman House, 2009), *Anabranch* (Wesleyan, 2004), and *By Reason of Breakings* (Georgia, 2002). He edited *Afterwards: Slovenian Writing 1945-1995* (White Pine, 1999).